VIOLENCE IN THE MEDIA

Other Books in the Current Controversies Series:

VIOLENCE IN THE MEDIA

David L. Bender, *Publisher*
Bruno Leone, *Executive Editor*

Katie de Koster, *Managing Editor*
Scott Barbour, *Senior Editor*

Carol Wekesser, *Book Editor*

CURRENT CONTROVERSIES

Cover Photo: Dan Habib / Impact Visuals

Library of Congress Cataloging-in-Publication Data

Violence in the media / Carol Wekesser, book editor.
    p. cm. — (Current controversies)
    Includes bibliographical references and index.
    ISBN 1-56510-236-3 (pbk.) : ISBN 1-56510-237-1 (lib.)
    1. Violence in mass media. I. Wekesser, Carol, 1963–   . II. Series.
P96.V5V56   1995
303.6—dc20
                                            94-43377
                                              CIP
                                              AC

© 1995 by Greenhaven Press, Inc., PO Box 289009, San Diego, CA 92198-9009
Printed in the U.S.A.

Contents

ness in children. In addition, these critics never consider the positive effect television may have on children.

Chapter 2: Should Media Violence Be Censored?

Chapter 3: Can the Media Effectively Regulate Violence in Their Products?

Chapter 5: Does Music Promote Violence?

Yes: Music Promotes Violence

Foreword

By definition, controversies are "discussions of questions in which opposing opinions clash" (Webster's Twentieth Century Dictionary Unabridged). Few would deny that controversies are a pervasive part of the human condition and exist on virtually every level of human enterprise. Controversies transpire between individuals and among groups, within nations and between nations. Controversies supply the grist necessary for progress by providing challenges and challengers to the status quo. They also create atmospheres where strife and warfare can flourish. A world without controversies would be a peaceful world; but it also would be, by and large, static and prosaic.

The Series' Purpose

The purpose of the Current Controversies series is to explore many of the social, political, and economic controversies dominating the national and international scenes today. Titles selected for inclusion in the series are highly focused and specific. For example, from the larger category of criminal justice, Current Controversies deals with specific topics such as police brutality, gun control, white collar crime, and others. The debates in Current Controversies also are presented in a useful, timeless fashion. Articles and book excerpts included in each title are selected if they contribute valuable, long-range ideas to the overall debate. And wherever possible, current information is enhanced with historical documents and other relevant materials. Thus, while individual titles are current in focus, every effort is made to ensure that they will not become quickly outdated. Books in the Current Controversies series will remain important resources for librarians, teachers, and students for many years.

In addition to keeping the titles focused and specific, great care is taken in the editorial format of each book in the series. Book introductions and chapter prefaces are offered to provide background material for readers. Chapters are organized around several key questions that are answered with diverse opinions representing all points on the political spectrum. Materials in each chapter include opinions in which authors clearly disagree as well as alternative opinions in which authors may agree on a broader issue but disagree on the possible solutions. In this way, the content of each volume in Current Controversies mirrors the mosaic of opinions encountered in society. Readers will quickly realize that there are many viable answers to these complex issues. By questioning each author's conclusions, students and casual readers can begin to develop the critical thinking skills so important to evaluating opinionated material.

Current Controversies is also ideal for controlled research. Each anthology in the series is composed of primary sources taken from a wide gamut of informational categories including periodicals, newspapers, books, United States and foreign government documents, and the publications of private and public organizations. Readers will find factual support for reports, debates, and research papers covering all areas of important issues. In addition, an annotated table of contents, an index, a book and periodical bibliography, and a list of organizations to contact are included in each book to expedite further research.

Perhaps more than ever before in history, people are confronted with diverse and contradictory information. During the Persian Gulf War, for example, the public was not only treated to minute-to-minute coverage of the war, it was also inundated with critiques of the coverage and countless analyses of the factors motivating U.S. involvement. Being able to sort through the plethora of opinions accompanying today's major issues, and to draw one's own conclusions, can be a complicated and frustrating struggle. It is the editors' hope that Current Controversies will help readers with this struggle.

*"On the one hand, media images may help to increase violence.
On the other, they may simply be an accurate reflection of societal
violence that has other causes."*

Introduction

The United States is a violent nation. In 1992, according to the Federal Bureau of Investigation (FBI), there were almost two million murders, rapes, robberies, and assaults. A U.S. Department of Justice report revealed that the U.S. violent crime rate is many times higher than that of other industrialized countries: murder, rape, and robbery occur four to nine times more frequently in the United States than in European countries.

This high rate of crime alarms the public. In a 1993 *Los Angeles Times* poll, crime was cited by respondents as the number one problem facing the nation. As Americans seek to understand the causes of their high rate of crime, one source often cited is violence in the media.

Those who believe that media violence is largely responsible for societal violence can cite many startling statistics and cases that support their view. For example, the American Psychological Association states that by seventh grade the average child has seen seven thousand murders and one hundred thousand acts of violence on television. Several murders and attacks have been connected to movies and television. For example, the movie *Taxi Driver* reportedly inspired John Hinckley's 1981 assassination attempt on then-president Ronald Reagan. To people such as S. Robert Lichter, codirector of the Center for Media and Public Affairs and coauthor of the book *Prime Time: How TV Portrays American Culture*, such statistics and cases prove that "there is more violence on television than ever, and the evidence of its harmful effects is compelling."

Yet, while such statistics and cases are alarming, the vast majority of American children who grow up viewing violent television programs and movies also grow up to be productive, normal, healthy adults. And while millions of Americans saw *Taxi Driver*, only one mentally ill young man used it as inspiration for attempted murder.

Columnist Carl Rowan writes that "movies and TV shows are not the primary teachers of violence and mayhem." Many factors influence an individual's propensity for "violence and mayhem." Sometimes violence is taught—for example, by an individual's culture or family. Sometimes it is inherited—for example, men in general have higher levels of the hormone testosterone than do women, and testosterone is linked to aggression.

Because the factors influencing an individual's propensity for violence are so numerous, isolating one factor such as media violence and labeling it the "cause" is almost impossible. But while media violence may not be the only or even the primary cause of societal violence, there is evidence showing a relationship between the two. On the one hand, media images may help to increase violence. On the other, they may simply be an accurate reflection of societal violence that has other causes. This is one of the many issues explored by the contributors in *Violence in the Media: Current Controversies*.

America is and has always been a violent nation, from its beginnings as a frontier to today. As British author T.H. White writes in his book *America at Last*, "Americans have a streak of lawlessness." To what extent television, movies, and music contribute to and exacerbate this "lawlessness" is an issue of much debate in a society concerned about violence.

Chapter 1

Does Media Violence
Affect Society?

CURRENT CONTROVERSIES

Chapter Preface

In the past forty years, sociologists have researched, government officials have studied, and many consumers have worried about how violence in the media affects society. In that time there have been more than three thousand reports on the effects of television viewing on Americans.

Most of the studies have concluded that there is some correlation between media violence and societal violence. For example, from 1960 to 1981 Leonard Eron tracked the viewing habits and lives of almost nine hundred children in one community. He found that the more television children watched at age eight, the greater the chance they would commit crimes as adults. Similarly, epidemiologist Brandon S. Centerwall found that as television viewing increased in the United States and Canada, so did the homicide rate.

Although the statistics seem convincing, there is still controversy concerning their meaning. Many contend that it is difficult to prove a cause-and-effect relationship between any two factors such as media violence and societal violence. Perhaps, rather than causing societal violence, violent media images simply reflect the increased violence in society. As writer Mike Males argues, "The biggest question media-violence critics can't answer is the most fundamental one: is it the *cause* or simply one of the many *symptoms*, of this unquestionably brutal age?" Others contend that it is simplistic to blame societal violence on the media, when in reality a multitude of factors are responsible for the problem. As U.S. senator Bill Bradley writes, "Violence . . . is a blaze fed by many fires."

So violence in the media might not be the sole or even the major cause of societal violence. But is it one factor in America's high rate of crime and excessive violence? And if so, should it be addressed by the government, media executives, or consumers? These are some of the questions discussed by the authors in the following chapter.

Media Violence Increases Violence in Society

by Carl M. Cannon

About the author: *Carl M. Cannon is the White House correspondent for the* Baltimore Sun *newspaper.*

Tim Robbins and Susan Sarandon implore the nation to treat Haitians with AIDS more humanely. Robert Redford works for the environment. Harry Belafonte marches against the death penalty.

Actors and producers seem to be constantly speaking out for noble causes far removed from their lives. They seem even more vocal and visible now that there is a Democrat [Bill Clinton] in the White House. But in the one area over which they have control—the excessive violence in the entertainment industry—Hollywood activists remain silent.

In the summer of 1993, Washington was abuzz with talk about the movie *Dave*, in which Kevin Kline stars as the acting president. But every time I saw an ad featuring Kline, the movie I couldn't get out of my head was *Grand Canyon*. There are two scenes in it that explain much of what has gone wrong in America.

Kline's character has a friend, played by Steve Martin, who is a producer of the B-grade, violent movies that Hollywood euphemistically calls "action" films. But after an armed robber shoots Martin's character in the leg, he has an epiphany.

"I can't make those movies any more," he decides. "I can't make another piece of art that glorifies violence and bloodshed and brutality. . . . No more exploding bodies, exploding buildings, exploding anything. I'm going to make the world a better place."

A month or two later, Kline calls on Martin at his Hollywood studio to congratulate him on the "new direction" his career has taken.

"What? Oh that," Martin says dismissively "Fuck that. That's over. I must have been delirious for a few weeks there."

He then gins up every hoary excuse for Hollywood-generated violence you've ever heard, ending with: "My movies reflect what's going on; they don't make what's going on."

Hollywood Shirks Its Responsibility

This is Hollywood's last line of defense for why it shows murder and mayhem on the big screen and the little one, in prime time and early in the morning, to children, adolescents, and adults:

We don't cause violence, we just report it.

In 1989, I joined the legion of writers, researchers, and parents who have tried to force Hollywood to confront the more disturbing truth. I wrote a series of newspaper articles on the massive body of evidence that establishes a direct cause-and-effect relationship between violence on television and violence in society.

The orchestrated response from the industry—a series of letters seeking to discredit me—was something to behold.

Because the fact is, on the one issue over which they have power, the liberals in Hollywood don't act like progressive thinkers; they act like, say, the National Rifle Association:

Guns don't kill people, people kill people.

We don't cause violence in the world, we just reflect it.

The first congressional hearings into the effects of television violence took place in 1954. Although television was still relatively new, its extraordinary marketing power was already evident. The tube was teaching Americans what to buy and how to act, not only in advertisements, but in dramatic shows, too.

Everybody from Hollywood producers to Madison Avenue ad men would boast about this power—and seek to utilize it on dual tracks: to make money and to remake society along better lines.

Because it seemed ludicrous to assert that there was only one area—the depiction of violence—where television did not influence behavior, the television industry came up with this theory: Watching violence is cathartic. A violent person might be sated by watching a murder.

The notion intrigued social scientists, and by 1956 they were studying it in earnest. Unfortunately, watching violence turned out to be anything but cathartic.

> *"Watching violence turned out to be anything but cathartic."*

In the 1956 study, one dozen four-year-olds watched a "Woody Woodpecker" cartoon that was full of violent images. Twelve other preschoolers watched "Little Red Hen," a peaceful cartoon. Then the children were observed. The children who watched "Woody Woodpecker" were more likely to hit other children, verbally accost their classmates, break toys, be disruptive, and engage in destructive behavior during free play.

For the next thirty years, researchers in all walks of the social sciences studied the question of whether television causes violence. The results have been stunningly conclusive.

"There is more published research on this topic than on almost any other social issue of our time," University of Kansas Professor Aletha C. Huston, chairwoman of the American Psychological Association's Task Force on Television and Society, told Congress in 1988. "Virtually all independent scholars agree that there is evidence that television can cause aggressive behavior."

Numerous Conclusive Studies

There have been some three thousand studies of this issue—eighty-five of them major research efforts—and they all say the same thing. Of the eighty-five major studies, the only one that failed to find a causal relationship between television violence and actual violence was paid for by NBC. When the study was subsequently reviewed by three independent social scientists, all three concluded that it actually did demonstrate a causal relationship.

Some highlights from the history of TV violence research:

• In 1973, when a town in mountainous western Canada was wired for television signals, University of British Columbia researchers observed first- and second-graders. Within two years, the incidence of hitting, biting, and shoving increased 160 percent in those classes.

> *"Virtually all independent scholars agree that there is evidence that television can cause aggressive behavior."*

• Two Chicago doctors, Leonard Eron and Rowell Huesmann, followed the viewing habits of a group of children for twenty-two years. They found that watching violence on television is the single best predictor of violent or aggressive behavior later in life, ahead of such commonly accepted factors as parents' behavior, poverty, and race.

"Television violence affects youngsters of all ages, of both genders, at all socioeconomic levels and all levels of intelligence," they told Congress in 1992. "The effect is not limited to children who are already disposed to being aggressive and is not restricted to this country."

• Fascinated by an explosion of murder rates in the United States and Canada that began in 1955, after a generation of North Americans had come of age on television violence, University of Washington Professor Brandon Centerwall decided to see if the same phenomenon could be observed in South Africa, where the Afrikaner-dominated regime had banned television until 1975.

He found that eight years after TV was introduced—showing mostly Hollywood-produced fare—South Africa's murder rate skyrocketed. His most telling finding was that the crime rate increased first in the white communities. This mirrors U.S. crime statistics in the 1950s and especially points the finger at television, because whites were the first to get it in both countries.

Bolder than most researchers, Centerwall argues flatly that without violent television programming, there might be as many as ten thousand fewer murders in the United States each year.

• In 1983, University of California, San Diego, researcher David P. Phillips wanted to see if there was a correlation between televised boxing matches and violence in the streets of America.

Looking at crime rates after every televised heavyweight championship fight from 1973 to 1978, Phillips found that the homicide rate in the United States rose by an average of

> *"Watching violence on television is the single best predictor of violent or aggressive behavior later in life."*

11 percent for approximately one week. Phillips also found that the killers were likely to focus their aggression on victims similar to the losing fighter: if he was white, the increased number of victims were mostly white. The converse was true if the losing fighter was black.

• In 1988, researchers Daniel G. Linz and Edward Donnerstein of the University of California, Santa Barbara, and Steven Penrod of the University of Wisconsin studied the effects on young men of horror movies and "slasher" films.

They found that depictions of violence, not sex, are what desensitizes people.

They divided male students into four groups. One group watched no movies, a second watched nonviolent, X-rated movies, a third watched teenage sexual-innuendo movies, and a fourth watched the slasher films *Texas Chainsaw Massacre*, *Friday the 13th Part 2*, *Maniac*, and *Toolbox Murders*.

All the young men were placed on a mock jury panel and asked a series of questions designed to measure their empathy for an alleged female rape victim. Those in the fourth group measured lowest in empathy for the specific victim in the experiment—and for rape victims in general.

Criminals Imitate Violence in TV, Movies

The anecdotal evidence is often more compelling than the scientific studies. Ask any homicide cop from London to Los Angeles to Bangkok if television violence induces real-life violence and listen carefully to the cynical, knowing laugh.

Ask David McCarthy, police chief in Greenfield, Massachusetts, why nineteen-year-old Mark Branch killed himself after stabbing an eighteen-year-old female college student to death. When cops searched his room they found ninety horror movies, as well as a machete and a goalie mask like those used by Jason, the grisly star of *Friday the 13th*.

Ask the families of thirty-five young men who committed suicide by playing Russian roulette after seeing the movie *The Deer Hunter*.

Ask George Gavito, a lieutenant in the Cameron County, Texas, sheriff's department, about a cult that sacrificed at least thirteen people on a ranch west of Matamoros, Mexico. The suspects kept mentioning a 1986 movie, *The Believ-*

ers, about rich families who engage in ritual sacrifice. "They talk about it like that had something to do with changing them," Gavito recalled later.

Ask Los Angeles Police Department lieutenant Mike Melton about Angel Regino of Los Angeles, who was picked up after a series of robberies and a murder in which he wore a blue bandanna and fedora identical to those worn by Freddy, the sadistic anti-hero of *Nightmare on Elm Street*. In case anybody missed the significance of his disguise, Regino told his victims that they would never forget him, because he was another Freddy Krueger.

Ask Britain Home Secretary Douglas Hurd, who called for further restrictions on U.S.-produced films after Michael Ryan of Hungerford committed Britain's worst mass murder in imitation of *Rambo*, massacring sixteen people while wearing a U.S. combat jacket and a bandoleer of ammunition.

Ask Sergeant John O'Malley of the New York Police Department about a nine-year-old boy who sprayed a Bronx office building with gunfire. The boy explained to the astonished sergeant how he learned to load his Uzi-like firearm: "I watch a lot of TV."

Or ask Manteca, California, police detective Jeff Boyd about thirteen-year-old Juan Valdez, who, with another teenager, went to a man's home, kicked him, stabbed him, beat him with a fireplace poker, and then choked him to death with a dog chain.

Why, Boyd wanted to know, had the boys poured salt in the victim's wounds?

"Oh, I don't know," the youth replied with a shrug. "I just seen it on TV."

Context Is Unimportant

Numerous groups have called, over the years, for curbing television violence: the National Commission on the Causes and Prevention of Violence (1969), the U.S. Surgeon General (1972), the Canadian Royal Commission (1976), the National Institute of Mental Health (1982), the U.S. Attorney General's Task Force on Family Violence (1984), the National Parents and Teachers Association (1987), and the American Psychological Association (1992).

During that time, cable television and movie rentals have made violence more readily available while at the same time pushing the envelope for network TV. But even leaving aside cable and movie rentals, a study of television programming from 1967 to 1989 showed only small ups and downs in violence, with the violent acts moving from one time slot to another but the overall violence rate remaining pretty steady—and pretty similar from network to network.

> *"Without violent television programming, there might be as many as ten thousand fewer murders in the United States each year."*

"The percent of prime-time programs using violence remains more than seven out of ten, as it has been for the entire twenty-two-year period," researchers

George Gerbner of the University of Pennsylvania Annenberg School for Communication and Nancy Signorielli of the University of Delaware wrote in 1990. For the past twenty-two years, they found, adults and children have been entertained by about sixteen violent acts, including two murders, in each evening's prime-time programming.

> *"Depictions of violence, not sex, are what desensitizes people."*

They also discovered that the rate of violence in children's programs is three times the rate in prime-time shows. By the age of eighteen, the average American child has witnessed at least eighteen thousand simulated murders on television.

By 1989, network executives were arguing that their violence was part of a larger context in which bad guys get their just desserts.

"We have never put any faith in mechanical measurements, such as counting punches or gunshots," said NBC's Alan Gerson. "Action and conflict must be evaluated within each specific dramatic context."

"Our policy," added Alfred R. Schneider of ABC, ". . . makes clear that when violence is portrayed [on TV], it must be reasonably related to plot development and character delineation."

Of course, what early-childhood experts could tell these executives is that children between the ages of four and seven simply make no connection between the murder at the beginning of a half-hour show and the man led away in handcuffs at the end. In fact, psychologists know that very young children do not even understand death to be a permanent condition.

A Toxic Substance

But all of the scientific studies and reports, all of the wisdom of cops and grief of parents have run up against Congress's quite proper fear of censorship. For years, Democratic Congressman Peter Rodino of New Jersey chaired the House Judiciary Committee and looked at calls for some form of censorship with a jaundiced eye. At a hearing in 1988, Rodino told witnesses that Congress must be a "protector of commerce."

"Well, we have children that we need to protect," replied Frank M. Palumbo, a pediatrician at Georgetown University Hospital and a consultant to the American Academy of Pediatrics. "What we have here is a toxic substance in the environment that is harmful to children."

Arnold Fege of the national PTA added, "Clearly, this committee would not protect teachers who taught violence to children. Yet why would we condone children being exposed to a steady diet of TV violence year after year?"

Finally there is a reason to hope for progress.

In the summer of 1993, Massachusetts Democrat Edward Markey, chair of the House Energy and Commerce subcommittee on telecommunications, said that Congress may require manufacturers to build TV sets with a computer chip so that parents could block violent programs from those their children could select.

He joins the fight waged by Senator Paul Simon, a liberal Democrat from Illinois. In 1984, Simon flipped on a hotel television set hoping to catch the late news. "Instead," he has recalled many times, "I saw a man being sawed in half with a chainsaw, in living color."

Simon was unsettled by the image and even more unsettled when he wondered what repeatedly looking at such images would do to the mind of a fourteen-year-old.

When he found out, he called television executives, who told him that violence sells and that they would be at a competitive disadvantage if they acted responsibly.

Why not get together and adopt voluntary guidelines? Simon asked.

Oh, that would be a violation of antitrust law, they assured him.

Simon called their bluff in 1990 by pushing through Congress a law that allowed a three-year moratorium on antitrust considerations so that the industry could discuss ways to jointly reduce violence.

Halfway through that time, however, they had done nothing, and an angry Simon denounced the industry on the Senate floor. With a push from some prominent industry figures, a conference was set.

> *"The rate of violence in children's programs is three times the rate in prime-time shows."*

In the spring of 1993, CBS broadcast group president Howard Stringer said his network was looking for ways to cut back on violence in its entertainment, because he was troubled by the cost to society of continuing business-as-usual.

"We must admit we have a responsibility," he said.

Jack Valenti, the powerful head of the Motion Picture Association of America, wrote to producers urging them to participate in the conference. "I think it's more than a bunch of talk," Simon said. "I think this conference will produce some results. I think the industry will adopt some standards."

Will Executives Respond?

The federal government, of course, possesses the power to regulate the airwaves through the FCC, and Simon and others believe that this latent power to control violence—never used—has put the fear of God in the producers. He also thinks some of them are starting to feel guilty.

"We now have more people in jail and prison per capita than any country that keeps records, including South Africa," Simon says. "We've spent billions putting people behind bars, and it's had no effect on the crime rate. None. People realize there have to be other answers, and as they've looked around, they have settled on television as one of them."

Maybe Simon is right. Maybe Hollywood executives will get together and make a difference.

Or maybe, like Steve Martin's character in *Grand Canyon*, producers and directors from New York to Beverly Hills will wake up after Simon's antitrust exemption expires, shake off the effects of their holiday hangovers, and when asked about their new commitment to responsible filmmaking, answer:

"What? Oh that. Fuck that. That's over. We must have been delirious for a few weeks there."

Media Violence Has Increased the Murder Rate

by Susan R. Lamson

About the author: *Susan R. Lamson is the director of federal affairs for the National Rifle Association's women's division.*

Turn on your TV virtually any time of any day and you can bring a carnival of murder, mayhem and bloodshed right into your living room. Maybe, like many Americans, you've grown accustomed to it and even expect it. But step back and look at this kaleidoscope of killing through the eyes of a child—and consider what role it's played for America's new generation of ultra-violent killers—and you see what a menace TV violence really is.

Televised mayhem is seen as a leading cause of America's epidemic of violent crime. It was the subject of May 12, 1993, hearings before the House Energy & Commerce Committee's Telecommunications & Finance subcommittee and the Senate Judiciary Committee's Constitution subcommittee. I represented the National Rifle Association (NRA) at the hearings and was joined by the nation's leading experts on human behavior and psychology to call for an end—or at least a reduction—of the broadcast brutality that's taking such a vicious toll on society.

As Dr. Brandon S. Centerwall, professor of epidemiology at the University of Washington, explained: "The U.S. national homicide rate has doubled since the 1950s. As a member of the Centers for Disease Control violence research team, my task was to determine why. A wide array of possible causes was examined—the 'baby boom' effect, trends in urbanization, economic trends, trends in alcohol abuse, the role of capital punishment, the effects of civil unrest, the availability of firearms, exposure to television.

"Over the course of seven years of investigation," Dr. Centerwall continued, "each of these purported causes was tested in a variety of ways to see whether it could be eliminated as a credible contributor to the doubling of rates of violence in the U.S. And, one by one, each of them was invalidated, except for television."

From Susan R. Lamson, "TV Violence: Does It Cause Real-Life Mayhem?" *American Rifleman*, July 1993. Reprinted with permission from the National Rifle Association of America.

If that's frightening to you, consider this: In his landmark 1989 study, Center-wall concluded "it is estimated that exposure to television is etiologically [causally] related to approximately one half of the homicides committed in the U.S., or approximately 10,000 homicides annually, and to a major proportion—perhaps one half—of rapes, assaults and other forms of inter-personal violence in the U.S."

Violence Sells

While not all agree with Centerwall's assessment of the problem's severity, few challenge his claim that Hollywood bloodshed *does* spill out from the screen and into our lives. As the American Psychological Association testified, the cause-and-effect link between TV violence and human aggression has been well established for nearly 20 years. But until recently the TV networks have been reluctant to change. That's why in 1990 Congress passed the Television Violence Act, that allowed the networks to cooperate and develop programming standards with which they and the public could live.

The problem is, violence sells. Media executives know it and profit from it. More viewers means higher ratings, which add up to more advertising dollars. So, as the National Institute of Mental Health has found, 80% of all television programs contain violent acts. But the violence is like a drug: viewers develop a tolerance for it, so media "pushers" give them steadily more.

Typically, prime-time programming has averaged 8 to 12 violent acts per hour. A recent study by the Annenberg School of Communications found violence in children's programming at an historic high—32 violent acts per hour. And a *TV Guide* study counted 1,845 acts of violence in 18 hours of viewing time, an average of 100 violent acts per hour, or one every 36 seconds.

While adults may see all this TV mayhem as just the latest "action entertainment," children don't get it. Psychologists agree that up to ages 3 and 4, children can't distinguish fact from fantasy on TV. For them, TV is a reflection of the world, and it's not a friendly place. Still, juvenile viewership is high. Children average nearly 4 hours of TV per day, and in the inner cities that increases to as many as 11 hours. Which means that in many cases, TV *is* the reality.

And this TV violence "addiction" is taking an increasingly grisly toll. FBI and census data show the homicide arrest rate for 17-year-olds more than doubled between 1985 and 1991, and the rates for 15- and 16-year-olds increased even faster. Psychologists point to several effects of televised

> *"Televised mayhem is seen as a leading cause of America's epidemic of violent crime."*

mayhem: Children are taught that society is normally violent. They become disproportionately frightened of being victimized and become less likely to help victims of crime. They also grow more aggressive and violent themselves.

Through the Television Violence Act, the major networks have agreed on a set of standards to reduce the level of gratuitous violence in their programs. But so far, there's been little change.

Ironically, 1993's congressional hearings on TV violence were in May—"sweeps month"—when the networks compete for the viewership ratings that determine their advertising profits for the year to come. Some critics are calling May 1993 one of the most violent sweeps months in TV history.

Empty Words

Whereas in years past, entertainment executives flatly refuted the dangers of TV violence, the network heads who testified during the May hearings were more receptive of change—or so they said. Still, their words somehow ring hollow, especially given the brutality in their "sweeps month" programming.

Howard Stringer, president of CBS, Warren Littlefield of NBC and Thomas S. Murphy of ABC all spoke at the congressional hearings. Stringer talked of his network's "principles," "seriousness," "responsibility" and "careful and extensive discussions"—yet there seems to be no end to the bloodshed. Then, in a *Washington Post* story days later, Stringer blamed firearms: "There are 200 million guns, 66 million handguns in America. That has a lot to do with violence, (the Washington, D.C., affiliate of Stringer's network rejected NRA's new commercial on the failings of the criminal justice system. The remarkable excuse given by CBS's affiliate was that the commercial "tends to inflame or incite.")

> *"The problem is, violence sells."*

Barring legislation, congressional hearings can't accomplish much without unified grassroots pressure from citizens. Ultimately, your letters, phone calls and faxes are the best ammunition in the fight to cut televised brutality and thus curb crime and safeguard your Second Amendment rights. When you see examples of pointless, gratuitous violence in your TV programming, write to the network executives and let them know how you feel.

Better yet, make a note of what products or services are advertised during violent programs, and voice your outrage to the leaders of those companies. You can get the proper names and addresses through your library's reference section. Excellent resources include *Standard and Poor's Register of Corporations, Directors and Executives*, Dun and Bradstreet's *Million Dollar Directory*, and *Moody's Manuals*.

In the end, only you—as a consumer, TV viewer and voter—can demand an end to the televised violence that's bloodying our society. If all NRA members and gun owners do their part in this fight, we *can* cut into the TV destruction that so gravely threatens both our children and our Bill of Rights.

Violence in TV News Promotes Violence Against Women

by Susan Douglas

About the author: *Susan Douglas is a columnist for the* Progressive *and the author of* Inventing American Broadcasting.

I am writing this at 1:00 A.M., long past my bedtime. I cannot sleep because of the nightly news. ABC featured an interview with a young woman from the former Yugoslavia who had been raped repeatedly by seven Serbian soldiers. But this was not the worst for her. She watched them take away her four-year-old daughter. When the little girl was returned, she was naked, blood streaming down between her legs.

I have a four-year-old daughter and I have been sickened and haunted all evening.

Later, on the local news, I watched the arraignment of a man who, in defiance of a restraining order, was accused of going to his former girlfriend's house and burning her alive, leaving her eleven-month-old child an orphan.

It seems that no matter how extravagant and profligate violence against women and their children becomes, an attitude of neglect and dismissal dominates the media discourse about what's to be done. Nowhere do we see the extent of the upper-middle-class, conservative, white, male bias of the media more clearly than when it comes to taking violence against women seriously.

"Private Stuff"?

Macho strutting by the neocon pundits sets the agenda for discussions about domestic and foreign policy. Fred "Blow-'em-Away" Barnes argued for "a preemptive strike" against nuclear facilities in North Korea that we aren't even sure exist. Barnes and the rest of the boys celebrated the arming of Nicaraguan contras, invading Panama, and bombing Iraq as necessary and patriotic. But

Susan Douglas, "Some Violence Is Not 'News,'" *The Progressive*, May 1993. Reprinted with permission.

save the women—especially the Muslim women of former Yugoslavia—from mass rape? Hey, wait a minute. The terrain is hilly and it's really complicated. Talk about domestic violence in the United States? Hey, that's private stuff.

This particular form of gender ideology masquerading as judgment and expertise sets the pundits' priorities about what is—and is not—important to place in the foreground each week. "Manly" topics, like Bill Clinton's budget proposals and what "we" should do about Russia, dominate the talk shows, while other issues of desperate concern to women and children are consistently ignored or deprecated.

Let's take two ongoing stories recently in the headlines: domestic violence in the United States and the proliferation of guns—both national crises of epidemic proportions. According to the FBI, a woman is battered by her husband or boyfriend every eighteen seconds in America; at least 1.13 million women reported being victims of domestic violence in 1991. Thirty per cent of female homicide victims are killed by their husbands or boyfriends. It turns out that Super Bowl Sunday is one of the worst days of the year to be a woman: To cite just one city, calls to battered women's shelters in the Los Angeles area doubled in the aftermath of the 1991 and 1992 Super Bowls.

To try to raise public awareness about the problem, Fairness and Accuracy in Reporting (FAIR) persuaded NBC to air a public-service announcement on domestic violence during the Super Bowl telecast. The

> *"Nowhere do we see the extent of the . . . male bias of the media more clearly than when it comes to taking violence against women seriously."*

backlash was swift and sure. *The Washington Post*, which had featured only two front-page stories on domestic violence in the previous four years, gave front-page space to Ken Rigle, who ridiculed the need for such a PSA and dismissed FAIR as a bunch of "causists [who] show up wherever the most TV lenses are focused." Alan Dershowitz, in an op-ed piece for the *Los Angeles Times*, derided FAIR activists as "zealots" and "self-proclaimed women's advocates" whose assertions about the relationship between Super Bowl Sunday and domestic violence were "false," a charge echoed by *The Wall Street Journal*. You will hardly be surprised to learn that Rush Limbaugh berated the PSA as "a bunch of feminist bilge." The TV pundits remained mute, as if domestic violence either doesn't exist or doesn't matter.

The News Media and Violence

You might think that the murder of Dr. David Gunn (a physician who performed abortions) by "right-to-life" zealot Michael Griffin and the armed confrontation, involving an arsenal of high-caliber weapons, between cult leader David Koresh and his followers and a battalion of law-enforcement officials in Waco, Texas, might get the pundits to discuss the new battle over guns. After all, during the same period, the New Jersey legislature fought back efforts to repeal the state's ban on semiautomatic assault weapons. In Virginia, where you used to be able to fill up a U-Haul in a one-stop shopping spree for guns, citizens are now restricted to purchasing one firearm per month. National Rifle Association–backed bills in Texas and Missouri would allow people to carry concealed weapons. Only Michael Wines, writing for the "Week in Review" section of *The New York Times*, put all these events together in an analysis of a critically important trend, the new war over guns. Once again, the TV pundits averted their gaze.

The sorry fact is that there is a sick, symbiotic relationship between violence and the news media. Conflict—and the more dramatic and lethal the better—is one of the fundamental criteria for whether a story is newsworthy. The proliferation of guns provides the news industry with an assured supply of stories. So does violence against women—as long as it's public, the woman is white, and there's a rape, mutilation, or murder involved.

This doesn't mean that all, or even most, journalists are opposed to gun control, or that they condone domestic violence. But it does mean they are implicated in a system that seeks to profit from a prurient and sensationalized representation of the victimization of women. More often than not, reporters focus on the woman who is battered, not the batterer, and ask why she doesn't leave instead of why he beats her. Each assault stands alone in the news, each woman a lonely, pathetic spectacle. Individually, their stories are welcome fodder for the news

> *"The sorry fact is that there is a sick, symbiotic relationship between violence and the news media."*

mill. But collectively, violence against women and children—and the mind-set that begets it—are ignored or minimized by the pundits as comparatively unimportant in the grand scheme of things.

Maybe this is why the pundits don't tell us that every single day in this country, fourteen children are killed with guns, or that America has three times as many animal shelters as it has shelters for battered women. And maybe it's one reason why trying to save little girls and their mothers, like the ones I saw on TV from Bosnia, is deemed foolhardy and impossible.

The Negative Impact of Media Violence on Society Is Exaggerated

by John Leonard

About the author: *John Leonard is a writer for the* Nation *and a television and movie critic who frequently appears on the CBS program* Sunday Morning.

Like a warrior-king of Sumer, daubed with sesame oil, gorged on goat, hefting up his sword and drum, Senator Ernest Hollings looked down November 23, 1993, from a ziggurat to lament, all over the Op-Ed page of *The New York Times*, the destruction of a fabled Ur: "If the TV and cable industries have no sense of shame, we must take it upon ourselves to stop licensing their violence-saturated programming."

Never Mind the Implications

Hollings, of course, is co-sponsor in the Senate, with Daniel Inouye, of a ban on any act of violence on television before, say, midnight. Never mind whether this is constitutional, or what it would do to the local news. Never mind, either, that in Los Angeles in August 1993, in the International Ballroom of the Beverly Hilton, in front of 600 industry executives, the talking heads—a professor here, a producer there, a child psychologist and a network veep for program standards—couldn't even agree on a definition of violence. (Is it only bad if it hurts or kills?) And they disagreed on which was worse, a "happy" violence that sugarcoats aggressive behavior or a "graphic" violence that at least suggests consequences. (How, anyway, does TV manage somehow simultaneously to *desensitize* and to *incite*?) Nor were they really sure what goes on in the dreamy heads of our children as they crouch in the dark to commune with the tube while their parents aren't around, if they have any. (*Roadrunner*? Beep-beep.) Nor does the infamous scarlet *V* "parent advisory" warning even apply to cartoons, afternoon soaps or Somalias.

John Leonard, "TV and the Decline of Civilization," *The Nation*, December 27, 1993. Reprinted with permission from *The Nation* magazine, © The Nation Company, L.P.

Never mind, because everybody agrees—even Robert Scheer in *The Nation* —that watching television causes antisocial behavior, especially among the children of the poor; that there seems to be more violent programming on the air now than there ever was before; that *Beavis and Butt-head* inspired an Ohio 5-year-old to burn down the family trailer; that in this blue druidic light we will have spawned generations of toadstools and traffids; and that fluoridated water causes brown teeth and Alaskan concentration camps.

Mostly Innocent Fare

In fact, there is less violence on network TV than there used to be; because of ratings, it's mostly sitcoms. The worst stuff is the Hollywood splatterflicks found on premium cable, which means the poor are less likely to be watching. Everywhere else on cable, not counting the Court channel or home shopping and not even to think about blood sports and Pat Buchanan, the fare is innocent to the point of stupefaction (Disney, Discovery, Family, Nickelodeon). That Ohio trailer wasn't even wired for cable, so the littlest firebird must have got his MTV elsewhere in the dangerous neighborhood. (And kids have been playing with matches since, at least, Prometheus. I recall burning down my very own bedroom when I was 5 years old. The fire department had to tell my mother.) Since the sixties, according to statistics cited by Douglas Davis in *The Five Myths of Television Power*, more Americans than ever before are going out to eat in restaurants, see films, plays and baseball games, visit museums, travel abroad, jog, even *read*. (A *Consumer Research Study on Book Purchasing* tells us that Americans in 1992 purchased 822 million adults books, an increase of 7 percent over 1991.) Watching TV, everybody does *something else* at the same time. While our children are playing with their Adobe Illustrators and Domark Virtual Reality Toolkits, the rest of us eat, knit, smoke, dream, read magazines, sign checks, feel sorry for ourselves, think about Hillary and plot shrewd career moves or revenge.

Actually watching TV, unless it's C-SPAN, is usually more interesting than the proceedings of Congress. Or what we read in hysterical books like Jerry Mander's *Four Arguments for the Elimination of Television*, or George Gilder's *Life After Television*, or Marie Winn's *The Plug-In Drug*, or Neal Postman's *Amusing Ourselves to Death*, or Bill McKibben's *The Age of Missing Information*. Or what we'll hear at panel discussions on censorship, where right-wingers worry about sex and left-wingers worry about violence. Or at symposiums on "The Apocalypse Trope in Television News" and seminars on "Postmodern Styles of Sadomasochism and Unkindness to Small Animals in Heavy Metal Music Videos." Or just lolling around an academic deepthink-tank, trading mantras like "frame analysis" (Erving Goffman), "wan-

> *"There is less violence on network TV than there used to be."*

ing of affect" (Fredric Jameson), "social facsimiles" (Kenneth Gergen), "pseudo realism" (T.W. Adorno), "violence profiles" (George Gerbner), "processed culture" (Richard Hoggart), "iconography of rooms" (Horace Newcomb), "narcoleptic joys" (Michael Sorkin) or "glass teat" (Harlan Ellison), not to mention "masturbation" (Michael Arlen, Allan Bloom, David Mamet). You'd think the talking furniture was somehow entropic, a heat-death of the culture.

No Evidence for TV's Link to Violence

Of *course* something happens to us when we watch TV: networks couldn't sell their millions of pairs of eyes to advertising agencies, nor would ad agencies buy more than $21 billion worth of commercial time each year, if speech (and sound, and motion) didn't somehow modify action. But what happens is far from clear and won't be much clarified by lab studies, however longitudinal, of habits and behaviors isolated from the larger feedback loop of a culture full of gaudy contradictions. The only country in the world that watches more television than we do is Japan, and you should see its snuff movies and pornographic comic books; but the Japanese are pikers compared with us when we compute per capita rates of rape and murder. Some critics in India tried to blame the recent rise in communal violence there on a state-run television series dramatizing the *Mahabharata*, but not long ago they were blaming Salman Rushdie, as in Bangladesh they have decided to blame the writer Taslima Nasrin. No Turk I

> *"Nobody normal watches TV the way Congressmen, academics, symposiasts and Bill McKibbens do."*

know of attributes skinhead violence to German TV. It's foolish to pretend that all behavior is mimetic, and that our only model is Spock or Brokaw. Or Mork and Mindy. Why, after so many years of *M*A*S*H*, weekly in prime time and nightly in reruns, aren't all of us out there hugging trees and morphing dolphins? Why, with so many sitcoms, aren't all of us comedians?

But nobody normal watches TV the way Congressmen, academics, symposiasts and Bill McKibbens do. We are less thrilling. For instance:

On March 3, 1993, a Wednesday, midway through the nine-week run of *Homicide* on NBC, in an episode written by Tom Fontana and directed by Martin Campbell, Baltimore detectives Bayliss (Kyle Secor) and Pembleton (Andre Braugher) had twelve hours to wring a confession out of "Arab" Tucker (Moses Gunn) for the strangulation and disemboweling of an 11-year-old girl. In the dirty light and appalling intimacy of a single claustrophobic room, with a whoosh of wind-sound like some dread blowing in from empty Gobi spaces, among maps, library books, diaries, junk food, pornographic crime-scene photographs and a single black overflowing ashtray, these three men seemed as nervous as the hand-held cameras—as if their black coffee were full of jumping beans, amphetamines and spiders; as if God Himself were jerking them around.

Pembleton, the black guy, played Good Cop. Bayliss, the white guy, played Bad Cop. Then, according to cop torque, they reversed themselves. This bearded "Arab," a peddler of fruits and vegetables, whose fiancée dumped him, whose horse died, whose barn burned down, was attacked in his Mad Dog alco-holism, his polygraph readings, his lapsed Baptist churchgoing and his sexuality. About to crack, he struck back. To Pembleton: "You hate nig-gers like me cuz you hate the inner nigger, you hate being who you re-ally are." And to Bayliss: "You got your dark side and it terrifies you. . . . You look into the mirror and all you see is an *amateur*." Finally the detectives got a confession, but not to the murder of the girl to whom "Arab," as if from the prodigal riches of Africa, gave peaches, pomegranates and an avocado: "I never touched her, not once." But 11-year-old Adena was nevertheless "the one great love" of this old man's wasted life.

> *"TV is always there for us, a twenty-four-hour user-friendly magic box."*

Well, you may think the culture doesn't really need another cop show. And, personally, I'd prefer a weekly series in which social problems are solved through creative nonviolence, after a Quaker meeting, by a collective of vege-tarian carpenters. But in a single hour, for which Tom Fontana eventually won an Emmy, I learned more about the behavior of fearful men in small rooms than from any number of better-known movies, plays and novels on the topic by the likes of Don DeLillo, Mary McCarthy, Alberto Moravia, Heinrich Böll and Doris Lessing.

A Twenty-Four-Hour Friend

This, of course, was an accident, as it usually is when those of us who watch television like normal people are startled in our expectations. We leave home expecting, for a lot of money, to be exalted, and almost never are. But staying put, slumped in an agnosticism about sentience itself, suspecting that our cable box is just another bad-faith credit card enabling us to multiply our opportuni-ties for disappointment, we are ambushed in our hebetude [lethargy]. And not so much by "event" television, like Ingmar Bergman's *Scenes From a Marriage*, originally a six-hour miniseries for Swedish television; or Marcel Ophuls's *The Sorrow and the Pity*, originally conceived for French television; or Rainer Werner Fassbinder's *Berlin Alexanderplatz*, commissioned by Ger-man television; or *The Singing Detective*; or *The Jewel in the Crown*. On the contrary, we've stayed home on certain nights to watch TV, the way on other nights we'll go out to a neighborhood restaurant, as if on Mondays we ordered in for laughs, as on Fridays we'd rather eat Italian. We go to television—mes-sage center, mission control, Big Neighbor, electronic Elmer's Glue-All—to look at Oscars, Super Bowls, moon shots, Watergates, Pearlygates, ayatollahs, dead kings, dead Kennedys; and also, perhaps, to experience some "virtual" community as a nation. But we also go because we are hungry, angry, lonely or tired, and TV is always there for us, a twenty-four-hour user friendly magic box grinding out narrative, novelty and distraction, news and laughs, snippets of high culture, remedial seriousness and vulgar celebrity, an incitement and a sedative, a place to celebrate and a place to mourn, a circus and a wishing well.

And suddenly Napoleon shows up, like a popsicle, on *Northern Exposure*, while Chris on the radio is reading Proust. Or it turns out *Law & Order* isn't laughing at the Mayflower Madam, not when her sorority sisters, who'd really rather eat buttered popcorn than go out and get paid for doing something *icky*, are also retail merchants of HIV. Or *Roseanne* is about lesbianism instead of bowling. Or *Picket Fences* has moved on, from serial bathers and elephant abuse to euthanasia and gay-bashing. Or between Inspector Morse and Zoe Wanamaker on *Mystery!* there is enough static cling to hydroelectrify the Yangtze. Or, on *The Young Indiana Jones Chronicles*, no sooner has young Indy finished consorting with Hemingways and Bolsheviks than he is being advised on his sexual confusions, in Vienna, by Dr. Freud and Dr. Jung.

The Importance of Narrative

Kurt Vonnegut on Showtime! David ("Masturbation") Mamet on TNT! Norman Mailer wrote the TV screenplay for *The Executioner's Song*, and Gore Vidal gave us *Lincoln* with Mary Tyler Moore as Mary Todd. In just the past five years, if I hadn't been watching television, I'd have missed *Tanner '88*, when Robert Altman and Garry Trudeau ran Michael Murphy for President of the United States; *A Very British Coup*, in which socialists and Mozart took over England; *My Name Is Bill W.*, with James Woods as the founding father of Alcoholics Anonymous; *Roe vs. Wade*, with Holly Hunter as a Supreme Court case; *The Final Days*, with Theodore Bikel as Henry Kissinger; *No Place Like Home*, where there wasn't one for Christine Lahti and Jeff Daniels, as there hadn't been for Jane Fonda in *The Dollmaker* and Mare Winningham in *God Bless the Child*; *Eyes on the Prize*, a home movie in two parts about America's second Civil War; *The Last Best Year*, with Mary Tyler Moore and Bernadette Peters learning to live with their gay sons and HIV; *Separate But Equal*, with Sidney Poitier as Thurgood Marshall; *Seize the Day*, with Robin Williams as a fictionalized Saul Bellow; *High Crimes and Misdemeanors*, the Bill Moyers special on Irangate and the scandal of our intelligence agencies; *Sessions*, where Billy Crystal used Elliott Gould to take on psychoanalysis; not

> *"We were a violent culture before TV, from Wounded Knee to the lynching bee."*

only Larry Gelbart's *Mastergate*, a deconstruction of the Reagan/Babar text, but also *Barbarians at the Gate*, his take on venture capitalism; Julie Dash's painterly meditation on Gullah culture off the Carolina coast, *Daughters of the Dust*; *The Caine Mutiny Court Martial*, set by Robert Altman on a basketball court; Evelyn Waugh's *Scoop*; Bette Midler's *Gypsy*; Graham Greene, John Up-dike, Philip Roth, Gloria Naylor, Arthur Miller and George Eliot, plus Paul Simon and Stephen Sondheim. Not to mention—guiltiest of all our secrets—those hoots without which any popular culture would be as tedious as a John Cage or an Anaïs Nin, like Elizabeth Taylor in *Sweet Bird of Youth* and the Redgrave sisters in a remake of *Whatever Happened to Baby Jane?*

What all this television has in common is narrative. Even network news—which used to be better than most newspapers before the bean counters started closing down overseas bureaus and the red camera lights went out all over Europe and Asia and Africa—is in the storytelling business. And what do we know about narrative? Well, we know what Christa Wolf told us, in *Cassandra:* "Only the advent of property, hierarchy, and patriarchy extracts a blood-red thread from the fabric of human life . . . and this thread is amplified at the expense of the web as a whole, at the expense of its uniformity. The blood-red thread is the narrative and struggle and victory of the heroes, or their doom. The plot is born." And what Don DeLillo told us in *Libra:* "There is a tendency of plots to move toward death . . . the idea of death is woven into the nature of every plot. A narrative plot no less than a conspiracy of armed men. The tighter the plot of a story, the more likely it will come to death."

In other words, either the Old Testament or the *Iliad* was the first Western, and the *Mahabharata* wasn't such a big improvement. Think of

> *"Children who are loved and protected long enough to grow up . . . don't riot in the streets."*

Troy and Masada as warm-ups for the Alamo. This frontier sex-and-violence stuff runs deep, from Hannibal to Attila to El Cid to Sergio Leone. What all Westerns have always been about is clout and turf and sexual property rights and how to look good dying. But so far no one in Congress has suggested banning narrative.

Learning from TV

Because I watch all those despised network TV movies, I know more about racism, ecology, homelessness, gun control, child abuse, gender confusion, date rape and AIDS than is dreamt of by, say, Katie Roiphe, the Joyce Maynard of Generation X, or than Hollywood has ever bothered to tell me, especially about AIDS. Imagine, Jonathan Demme's *Philadelphia* opened in theaters around the country [only] after at least a dozen TV movies on the subject that I can remember without troubling my hard disk. And I've learned something else, too:

We were a violent culture before TV, from Wounded Knee to the lynching bee, and we'll be one after all our children have disappeared by video game into the pixels of cyberspace. Before TV, we blamed public schools for what went wrong with the Little People back when classrooms weren't overcrowded in buildings that weren't falling down in neighborhoods that didn't resemble

Beirut, and whose fault is that? *The A-Team*? We can't control guns, or drugs, and each year 2 million American women are assaulted by their male partners, who are usually in an alcoholic rage, and whose fault is that? *Miami Vice*? The gangs that menace our streets aren't home watching Cinemax, and neither are the sociopaths who make bonfires, in our parks, from our homeless, of whom there are at least a million, a supply-side migratory tide of the deindustrialized and dispossessed, of angry beggars, refugee children and catatonic nomads, none of them traumatized by *Twin Peaks*. So cut Medicare, kick around the Brady bill and animadvert Amy Fisher movies. But children who are loved and protected long enough to grow up to have homes and respect and lucky enough to have jobs don't riot in the streets. Ours is a tantrum culture that measures everyone by his or her ability to produce wealth, and morally condemns anybody who fails to prosper, and now blames Burbank for its angry incoherence. Why not recessive genes, angry gods, lousy weather? The mafia, the zodiac, the *Protocols of the Elders of Zion*? Probability theory, demonic possession, Original Sin? George Steinbrenner? Sunspots?

Evidence Connecting Media Violence to Real Violence Is Weak

by Brian Siano

About the author: *Brian Siano is a writer and researcher in Philadelphia. He is a regular columnist for the* Humanist.

Here's the scene: Bugs Bunny, Daffy Duck, and a well-armed Elmer Fudd are having a stand-off in the forest. Daffy the rat-fink has just exposed Bugs' latest disguise, so Bugs takes off the costume and says, "That's right, Doc, I'm a wabbit. Would you like to shoot me now or wait until we get home?"

"Shoot him now! Shoot him now!" Daffy screams.

"You keep out of this," Bugs says. "He does not have to shoot you now."

"He does *so* have to shoot me now!" says Daffy. Full of wrath, he storms up to Elmer Fudd and shrieks. "And I *demand* that you shoot me now!"

Now, if you *aren't* smiling to yourself over the prospect of Daffy's beak whirling around his head like a roulette wheel, stop reading right now. This one's for a very select group: those evil degenerates (like me) who want to corrupt the unsullied youth of America by showing them violence on television.

Wolves' heads being conked with mallets in Tex Avery's *Swing Shift Cinderella*. Dozens of dead bodies falling from a closet in *Who Killed Who?* A sweet little kitten seemingly baked into cookies in Chuck Jones' *Feed the Kitty*. And best of all, Wile E. Coyote's unending odyssey of pain in *Fast and Furious* and *Hook, Line, and Stinker*. God, I love it. The more explosions, crashes, gunshots, and defective ACME catapults there are, the better it is for the little tykes.

Shocked? Hey, I haven't even gotten to *The Three Stooges* yet.

Concerned Politicians

The villagers are out hunting another monster—the Frankenstein of TV violence. Senator Paul Simon's hearings in early August 1993 provoked a fresh round of arguments in a debate that's been going on ever since the first round of violent kids' shows—*Sky King*, *Captain Midnight*, and *Hopalong Cassidy*— were on the air. More recently, Attorney General Janet Reno has taken a hard line on TV violence. "We're fed up with excuses," she told the Senate, arguing that "the regulation of violence is constitutionally permissible" and that, if the networks don't do it, "government should respond." Reno herself presents a fine example, given her rotisserielike tactics with the Branch Davidian sect in Waco, Texas, in April 1993, or her medieval record

> *"The more explosions, crashes, gunshots, and defective ACME catapults there are, the better it is for the little tykes."*

on prosecuting "satanic ritual abuse" cases in Florida. (At least she wasn't as befuddled as Senator Ernest Hollings, who kept referring to *Beavis and Butt-head* as *Buffcoat and Beaver*.)

Simon claims to have become concerned with this issue because, a few years ago, he turned on the TV in his hotel room and was treated to the sight of a man being hacked apart with a chainsaw. (From his description, it sounds like the notorious scene in Brian de Palma's *Scarface*—itself censored to avoid an X-rating— but Simon never said what network, cable, or pay-per-view channel he saw it on.) This experience prompted him to sponsor a three-year antitrust exemption for the networks, which was his way of encouraging them to voluntarily "clean house." But at the end of that period, the rates of TV violence hadn't changed enough to satisfy him, so Simon convened open hearings on the subject in 1993.

The Issue of Ownership

If Simon was truly concerned with the content of television programming, the first question that comes to mind is why he gave the networks an antitrust exemption in the first place. Thanks to Reagan-era deregulation, ownership of the mass media has become steadily more concentrated in the hands of fewer and fewer corporations. For example, the Federal Communications Commission used to have a "7-and-7" rule, whereby no company was allowed to own more than 7 radio and 7 television stations. In 1984, this was revised to a "12-and-12-and-12" rule: 12 FM radio stations, 12 AM radio stations, and 12 TV stations. It's a process outlined by Ben Bagdikian in his fine book *The Media Monopoly*. The net result is a loss of dissident, investigative, or regional voices; a mass media that questions less; and a forum for public debate that includes only the powerful.

This process could be impeded with judicious use of antitrust laws and stricter FCC controls—a return to the "7-and-7" rule, perhaps. But rather than hold hearings on this subject—a far greater threat to the nation's political well-being than watching *Aliens* on pay-per-view—Simon gave the networks a three-year *exemption* from antitrust legislation.

There's a reason we should be concerned about this issue of media ownership:

television influences people. That's its *job*. Advertisers don't spend all that money on TV commercials because they have no impact. Corporations don't dump money into PBS shows like *The McLaughlin Group* or *Firing Line* unless they are getting their point across. *Somebody* is buying stuff from the Home Shopping Network and keeping Rush Limbaugh's ratings up. Then, too, we all applaud such public-service initiatives as "Don't Drink and Drive" ads, and I think most of us would be appalled if Donatello of the *Teenage Mutant Ninja Turtles* lit up a Marlboro or chugged a fifth of Cutty Sark. So it's not unreasonable to wonder whether violent television might be encouraging violent behavior.

The debate becomes even more impassioned when we ask how children might be affected. The innocent, trusting little tykes are spending hours bathed in TV's unreal colors, and their fantasy lives are inhabited by such weirdos as Wolverine and Eek the Cat. Parents usually want their kids to grow up sharing their ideals and values, or at least to be well behaved and obedient. Tell parents that their kids are watching *Beavis and Butt-head* in their formative years and you set off some major alarms.

Snobbish Hysteria

There are also elitist, even snobbish, attitudes toward pop culture that help to rationalize censorship. One is that the corporate, mass-market culture of TV isn't important enough or "art" enough to deserve the same free-speech protection as James Joyce's *Ulysses* or William Burroughs' *Naked Lunch*. The second is that rational, civilized human beings are supposed to be into Shakespeare and Scarlatti, not Pearl Jam and *Beavis and Butt-head*. Seen in this "enlightened" way, the efforts of Paul Simon are actually for *our own good*. And so we define anything even remotely energetic as "violent," wail about how innocent freckle-faced children are being defiled by such fare as *NYPD Blue*, and call for a Council of Certified Nice People who will decide what the rest of us get to see. A 1993 *Mother Jones* article by Carl Cannon took just this hysterical tone, citing as proof "some three thousand research studies of this issue."

Actually, there aren't 3,000 studies. In 1984, the *Psychological Bulletin* published an overview by Jonathan Freedman of research on the subject. Referring to the "2,500 studies" fig-

> *"Elitist, even snobbish, attitudes toward pop culture . . . help to rationalize censorship."*

ure bandied about at the time (it's a safe bet that 10 years would inflate this figure to 3,000), Freedman writes:

> The reality is more modest. The large number refers to the complete bibliography on television. References to television and aggression are far fewer, perhaps around 500. . . . The actual literature on the relation between television violence and aggression consists of fewer than 100 independent studies, and the majority of these are laboratory experiments. Although this is still a substantial

body of work, it is not vast, and there are only a small number of studies dealing specifically with the effects of television violence outside the laboratory.

The bulk of the evidence for a causal relationship between television violence and violent behavior comes from the research of Leonard Eron of the University of Illinois and Rowell Huesmann of the University of Michigan. Beginning in 1960, Eron and his associates began a large-scale appraisal of how aggression develops in children and whether or not it persists into adulthood. (The question of television violence was, originally, a side issue to the long-term study.) Unfortunately, when the popular press writes about Eron's work, it tends to present his methodology in the simplest of terms: *Mother Jones* erroneously stated that his study "followed the viewing habits of a group of children for twenty-two years." It's this sort of sloppiness, and overzealousness to prove a point, that keeps people from understanding the issues or raising substantial criticisms. Therefore, we must discuss Eron's work in some detail.

> *"Aggressive kids who turn into aggressive adults like aggressive television. But this is a correlation; it is not proof of a causal influence."*

Parents and Aggressiveness in Children

The first issue in Eron's study was how to measure aggressiveness in children. Eron's "peer-nominated index" followed a simple strategy: asking each child in a classroom questions about which kids were the main offenders in ten different categories of classroom aggression (that is, "Who pushes or shoves children?"). The method is consistent with other scales of aggression, and its one-month test/retest reliability is 91 percent. The researchers also tested the roles of four behavioral dimensions in the development of aggression: *instigation* (parental rejection or lack of nurturance), *reinforcement* (punishment versus reward), *identification* (acquiring the parents' behavior and values), and *sociocultural norms*.

Eron's team selected the entire third-grade population of Columbia County, New York, testing 870 children and interviewing about 75 to 80 percent of their parents. Several trends became clear almost immediately. Children with less nurturing parents were more aggressive. Children who more closely identified with either parent were less aggressive. And children with low parental identification who were punished tended to be *more* aggressive (an observation which required revision of the behavioral model).

Ten years later, Eron and company tracked down and reinterviewed about half of the original sample. (They followed up on the subjects in 1981 as well.) Many of the subjects—now high-school seniors—demonstrated a persistence in aggression over time. Not only were the "peer-nominated" ratings roughly consistent with the third-grade ratings, but the more aggressive kids were three times as likely to have a police record by adulthood.

Eron's team also checked for the influences on aggression which they had previously noted when the subjects were eight. The persistent influences were parental identification and socioeconomic variables. Some previously important influences (lack of nurturance, punishment for aggression) didn't seem to affect the subjects' behavior as much in young adulthood. Eron writes of these factors:

> Their effect is short-lived and other variables are more important in predicting later aggression. Likewise, contingencies and environmental conditions can change drastically over 10 years, and thus the earlier contingent response becomes irrelevant.

It's at this stage that Eron mentions television as a factor:

> One of the best predictors of how aggressive a young man would be at age 19 was the violence of the television programs he preferred when he was 8 years old. Now, because we had longitudinal data, we could say with more certainty, on the basis of regression analysis, partial correlation, path analysis, and so forth, that there indeed was a cause-and-effect relation. *Continued research, however, has indicated that the causal effect is probably bidirectional: Aggressive children prefer violent television, and the violence on television causes them to be more aggressive.* [italics added]

Before we address the last comment, I should make one thing clear. Eron's research is sound. The methods he used to measure aggression are used by social scientists in many other contexts. His research does not ignore such obvious factors as the parents' socioeconomic status. And, as the above summary makes clear, Eron's own work makes a strong case for the positive or negative influence of parents in the development of their children's aggressiveness.

> *"Assuming a causal influence, television might be responsible for 5 percent of the violence in society. At* most.*"*

Causal Effect?

Now let's look at this "causal effect" business. Eron's data reveals that aggressive kids who turn into aggressive adults like aggressive television. But this is a correlation; it is not proof of a causal influence. If aggressive kids liked eating strawberry ice cream more often than the class wusses did, that too would be a predictor, and one might speculate on some anger-inducing chemical in strawberries.

Of course, the relation between representational violence and its influence on real life isn't as farfetched as that. The problem lies in determining precisely the nature of that relation, as we see when we look at the laboratory studies conducted by other researchers. Usually, the protocol for these experiments involves providing groups of individuals with entertainment calibrated for violent content, and studying some aspect of behavior after exposure—response to a behavioral test, which toys the children choose to play with, and so forth. But the results of these tests have been somewhat mixed. Sometimes the results are at variance with other studies, and many have methodological problems. For example, which "violent" entertainment is chosen? Bugs Bunny and the *Teenage Mutant Ninja Turtles* present action in very different contexts, and in one study, the Adam West *Batman* series was deemed nonviolent, despite those *Pow! Bam! Sock!* fistfights that ended every episode.

Inconsistent Results from Studies

Many of the studies report that children do demonstrate higher levels of interpersonal aggression shortly after watching violent, energetic entertainment. But a 1971 study by Feshbach and Singer had boys from seven schools watch preassigned violent and nonviolent shows for six weeks. The results were not constant from school to school—and the boys watching the *nonviolent* shows tended to be more aggressive. Another protocol, carried out in Belgium as well as the United States, separated children into cottages at an institutional school and exposed certain groups to violent films. Higher aggression was noted in *all* groups after the films were viewed, but it returned to a near-baseline level after a week or so. (The children also rated the less violent films as less exciting, more boring, and sillier than the violent films—indicating that maybe kids *like* a little rush now and then.) Given the criticisms of the short-term-effects studies, and the alternate interpretations of the longitudinal studies, is this matter really settled?

Eron certainly thinks so. Testifying before Simon's committee, he declared that "the scientific debate is over" and called upon the Senate to reduce TV violence. His statement did not include any reference to such significant factors as parental identification—which, as his own research indicates, can change the way children interpret physical punishment. And even though Rowell Huesmann concurred with Eron in similar testimony before a House subcommittee, Huesmann's 1984 study of 1,500 youths in the United States, Finland, Poland, and Australia argued that, assuming a causal influence, television might be responsible for 5 percent of the violence in society. At *most*.

This is where I feel one has to part company with Leonard Eron. He is one of the most respected researchers in his field, and his work points to an imperative for parents in shaping and sharing their children's lives. But he has lent his considerable authority to such diversionary efforts as Paul Simon's and urged us to address, by questionable means, what only *might* be causing a tiny portion of real-life violence.

> *"The vast majority of people don't take a movie or a TV show as a license to kill."*

Some of Eron's suggestions for improving television are problematic as well. In his Senate testimony, Eron proposed restrictions on televised violence from

6:00 A.M. to 10:00 P.M.—which would exclude pro football, documentaries about World War II, and even concerned lawperson Janet Reno's proudest moments. Or take Eron's suggestion that, in televised drama, "perpetrators of violence should not be rewarded for violent acts." I don't know what shows Eron's been watching, but all of the cop shows I remember usually ended with the bad guys getting caught or killed. And when Eron suggests that "gratuitous violence that is not necessary to the plot should be reduced or abandoned," one has to ask just *who* decides that it's "not necessary"? Perhaps most troubling is Eron's closing statement:

> For many years now Western European countries have had monitoring of TV and films for violence by government agencies and have *not* permitted the showing of excess violence, especially during child viewing hours. And I've never heard complaints by citizens of those democratic countries that their rights have been violated. If something doesn't give, we may have to institute some such monitoring by government agencies here in the U.S.A. If the industry does not police itself, then there is left only the prospect of official censorship, distasteful as this may be to many of us.

The most often-cited measure of just how violent TV programs are is that of George Gerbner, dean of the Annenberg School of Communications at the University of Pennsylvania. Few of the news stories about TV violence explain how this index is compiled, the context in which Gerbner has conducted his studies, or even some criticisms that could be raised.

> *"I'd have no problems with showing a 10-year-old* **Jurassic Park,** *because I know how much he or she would love it."*

Gerbner's view of the media's role in society is far more nuanced than the publicity given the violence profile may indicate. He sees television as a kind of myth-structure/religion for modern society. Television dramas, situation comedies, news shows, and all the rest create a shared culture for viewers, which "communicates much about social norms and relationships, about goals and means, about winners and losers." One portion of Gerbner's research involves compiling "risk ratios" in an effort to discern which minority groups—including children, the aged, and women—tend to be the victims or the aggressors in drama. This provides a picture of a pecking order within society (white males on top, no surprise there) that [as of 1993] has remained somewhat consistent over the 20-year history of the index.

Defining Violence

In a press release accompanying the 1993 violence index, Gerbner discusses his investigations of the long-term effects of television viewing. Heavy viewers were more likely to express feelings of living in a hostile world. Gerbner adds, "Violence is a demonstration of power. It shows who can get away with what against whom."

In a previous violence index compiled for cable-television programs, violence is defined as a "clear-cut and overt episode of physical violence—hurting or killing or the threat of hurting and/or killing—in any context." An earlier defi-

> *"I'd rather not lose **decent** shows that use violence for good reason."*

nition reads: "The overt expression of physical force against self or other compelling action against one's will on pain of being hurt or killed, or actually hurting or killing." These definitions have been criticized for being too broad; they encompass episodes of physical comedy, depiction of accidents in dramas, and even violent incidents in documentaries. They also include zany cartoon violence; in fact, the indexes for Saturday-morning programming tend to be substantially higher than the indexes for prime-time programming. Gerbner argues that, since he is analyzing cultural norms and since television entertainment is a deliberately conceived expression of these norms, his definition serves the purposes of his study.

No Measure of Actual Violent Content

The incidents of violence (total number = R) in a given viewing period are compiled by Gerbner's staff. Some of the statistics are easy to derive, such as the percentage of programs with violence, the number of violent scenes per hour, and the actual duration of violence, in minutes per hour. The actual violence index is calculated by adding together the following stats:

$\%P$— the *percentage* of programs in which there is violence;

$2(R/P)$— twice the number of violent episodes per program;

$2(R/H)$— twice the number of violent episodes per *hour*;

$\%V$— percentage of *leading characters* involved in violence, either as victim or perpetrator; and

$\%K$— percentage of leading characters involved in an actual *killing*, either as victim or perpetrator.

But if these are the factors used to compile the violence profile, it's difficult to see how they can provide a clear-cut mandate for the specific content of television drama. For example, two of the numbers used are averages; why are they arbitrarily doubled and then added to percentages? Also, because the numbers are determined by a definition which explicitly separates violence from dramatic context, the index says little about actual television content outside of a broad, overall gauge. One may imagine a television season of nothing but slapstick comedy with a very high violence profile.

This is why the violence profile is best understood within the context of Gerbner's wider analysis of media content. It does not lend itself to providing specific conclusions or guidelines of the sort urged by Senator Paul Simon. (It is important to note that, even though Simon observed little change in prime-time violence levels during his 3-year antitrust exemption, the index for all 3 of those years was *below* the overall 20-year score.)

Finally, there's the anecdotal evidence—loudly trumpeted as such by Carl Cannon in *Mother Jones*—where isolated examples of entertainment-inspired violence are cited as proof of its pernicious influence. Several such examples have turned up. A sequence was edited out of the film *The Good Son* in which Macaulay Culkin drops stuff onto a highway from an overhead bridge. (As we all know, nobody ever did this before the movie came out.) The film *The Program* was re-edited when some kids were killed imitating the film's characters, who "proved their courage" by lying down on a highway's dividing line. Perhaps most notoriously, in October 1993 a four-year-old Ohio boy set his family's trailer on fire, killing his younger sister; the child's mother promptly blamed MTV's *Beavis and Butt-head* for setting a bad example. But a neighbor interviewed on CNN reported that the family didn't even have cable television and that the kid had a local rep as a pyromaniac months before. This particular account was not followed up by the national media, which, if there were no enticing *Beavis and Butt-head* angle, would never have mentioned this fire at a low-income trailer park to begin with.

Atypical Cases

Numerous articles about media-inspired violence have cited similar stories— killers claiming to be Freddy Kreuger, kids imitating crimes they'd seen on a cop show a few days before, and so forth. In many of these cases, it is undeniably true that the person involved took his or her inspiration to act from a dramatic presentation in the media—the obvious example being John Hinckley's fixation on the film *Taxi Driver*. [Hinckley attempted to assassinate President Ronald Reagan in March 1981, claiming he did it because of his infatuation with *Taxi Driver* star Jodie Foster.] (Needless to say, Bible-inspired crimes just don't attract the ire of Congress.) But stories of media-inspired violence are striking mainly because they're so *atypical* of the norm; the vast majority of people don't take a movie or a TV show as a license to kill. Ironically, it is the *abnormality* of these stories that ensures they'll get widespread dissemination and be remembered long after the more mundane crimes are forgotten.

> *"Shows like **Star Trek** . . . can give kids a sense of adventure while teaching them about such qualities as courage, bravery, and heroism."*

Of course, there are a few crazies out there who will be unfavorably influenced by what they see on TV. But even assuming that somehow the TV show (or movie or record) shares some of the blame, how does one predict what future crazies will take for inspiration? What guidelines would ensure that people write, act, or produce something that *will not upset a psychotic?* Not only is this a ridiculous demand, it's insulting to the public as well. We would all be treated as potential murderers in order to gain a hypothetical 5 percent reduction in violence.

In crusades like this—where the villagers pick up their torches and go hunting after Frankenstein—people often lose sight of what they're defending. I've read reams of statements from people who claim to know what television does to kids; but what do *kids* do with television? Almost none of what I've read gives kids any credit for thinking. None of these people seems to remember what being a kid is like.

When *Jurassic Park* was released, there was a huge debate over whether or not children should be allowed to see it. Kids like to see dinosaurs, people argued, but this movie might scare them into catatonia. There was even the suspicion that Steven Spielberg and company were being sneaky and underhanded by making a film about dinosaurs that was terrifying. These objections were actually taken seriously. But kids like dinosaurs because they're big, look really weird, and scare the hell out of everything around them. Dinosaurs *kick ass*. What parent would tell his or her child that dinosaurs were *cute?* (And how long have these "concerned parents" been *lying* to their kids about the most fearsome beasts ever to shake the earth?)

Along the same lines, what kid hasn't tried to gross out everyone at the dinner table by showing them his or her chewed-up food? Or tried using a magnifying glass on an anthill on a hot day? Or clinically inspected the first dead animal he or she ever came across? Sixty years ago, adults were terrified of *Frankenstein* and fainted at the premiere of *King Kong*. But today, *Kong* is regarded as a fantasy story, *Godzilla* can be shown without the objections of child psychologists, and there are breakfast cereals called Count Chocula and Frankenberry. Sadly, there are few adults who seem to remember how they identified more with the monsters. Who wanted to be one of those stupid villagers waving torches at Frankenstein? That's what our *parents* were like.

> *"Kids want to stick up for themselves . . . against a world made by adults."*

But it's not just an issue of kids' liking violence, grossness, or comic-book adventure. About 90 percent of the cartoon shows I watched as a child were the mass-produced sludge of the Hanna-Barbera Studios—like *Wacky Races*, *The Jetsons*, and *Scooby Doo, Where Are You?* I can't remember a single memorable moment from any of them. But that Bugs Bunny sequence at the beginning of this article (from *Rabbit Seasoning*, 1952, directed by Chuck Jones) was done from memory, and I have no doubt that it's almost verbatim.

I know that, even at the age of eight or nine, I had some rudimentary aesthetic sense about it all. There was something hip and complex about the Warner Bros. cartoons, and some trite, insulting *sameness* to the Hanna-Barbera trash, although I couldn't quite understand it then. Bugs Bunny clearly wasn't made for kids according to some study on social-interaction development. Bugs Bunny was meant to make adults laugh as much as children. Kids can also enjoy entertainment ostensibly created for adults—in fact, that's often the most rewarding kind. I had no trouble digesting *Jaws*, James Bond, and Clint Eastwood "spaghetti westerns" in my preteen years. And I'd have no problems with showing a 10-year-old *Jurassic Park*, because I know how much he or she would love it.

Another example: Ralph Bakshi's brilliant *Mighty Mouse* series was canceled after the Reverend Donald Wildmon claimed it showed the mouse snorting coke. Kids don't organize mass write-in campaigns, and I hate to see them lose something wonderful just because some officious crackpot decides it was corrupting their morals. Perhaps aspartame-drenched shows like *Barney and Friends* [about a loving purple dinosaur] or *Widget* (a purple, spermy little alien who can do magic) encourage children to be good citizens, but they also encourage kids to be docile and unimaginative—just the sort of "good citizens" easily manipulated by the likes of Wildmon.

I don't enjoy bad television with lots of violence, but I'd rather not lose *decent* shows that use violence for good reason. Shows like *Star Trek*, *X-Men*, or the spectacular *Batman: The Animated Series* can give kids a sense of adventure while teaching them about such qualities as courage, bravery, and heroism. Even better, a healthy and robust spirit of irreverence can be found in Bugs Bunny, *Ren and Stimpy*, and *Tiny Toons*. Some of these entertainments—like adventure stories and comic books of the past—can teach kids how to be really *alive*.

Irreverence Is Vital

Finally, if we must have a defense against the pernicious influence of the mass media, it cannot be from the Senate's legislation or the pronouncements of social scientists. It must begin with precisely the qualities I described above—especially irreverence. One good start is Comedy Central's *Mystery Science Theater 3000*, where the main characters, forced to watch horrendous movies, fight back by heckling them. Not surprisingly, children love the show, even though most of the jokes go right over their curious little heads. They recognize a kindred spirit in *MST 3000*. Kids want to stick up for themselves, maybe like Batman, maybe like Bugs Bunny, or even like Beavis and Butthead—but always against a world made by adults.

You know, *adults*—those doofuses with the torches, trying to burn up Frankenstein in the old mill.

Media Violence May Not Harm Children

by Patrick Cooke

About the author: *Patrick Cooke is a writer.*

Academia's dire warnings about the dangers of watching the tube have always been an easy sell. But with Senator Paul Simon hinting darkly at Government censorship unless the industry does a better job of policing itself, the ante has been raised. The question is: do TV researchers know what they're talking about?

Since the late 1940's, there have been more than 3,000 reports on the effect on viewers of watching television, and TV research itself has become a cottage industry. Most of the conclusions have been grim; many have been baffling. Here are some of the findings of the past few decades: TV leads to hyperactivity in children; TV makes children passive. TV isolates viewers; TV comforts the lonely. TV drives families apart; TV brings families together.

Not even the Public Broadcasting Service has been spared. In 1975, when researchers noticed 2-year-old children obsessively reciting numbers and letters, one study cautioned parents about a new disorder called the "Sesame Street Hazard."

In 1989, the Department of Education financed the most extensive survey to date of the research on childhood development and TV. It concluded that a disturbing amount of scholarship had been slipshod or influenced by a prevailing attitude that TV is harmful.

Assumptions May Be Wrong

Despite the difficulty of obtaining reliable information on how television influences people, some beliefs, particularly about violence, are as persistent as *Cheers* reruns. The National Coalition on Television Violence, for example, has for years asserted that murders and rapes are more likely to occur because of TV violence. According to the organization, "It increases the chances that you will be mugged in the street or have your belongings stolen."

Many Americans agree with this conclusion; the link between mayhem on TV and a real-life violent society, after all, seems to make sense. But consider this possible area for research: Why doesn't anyone ever talk about the many occasions when people are nice to one another on TV? What effect has that had?

Much of the hand-wringing at [an August 1993] Beverly Hills conference [on violence in television] centered on the sheer volume of brutality young people witness on TV and how, at the very least, such incidents desensitize them to real violence. But if teenagers have seen 18,000 TV murders by the age of 16, as one study estimated, isn't it possible, given the popularity of shows like *Fresh Prince of Bel Air*, *Brooklyn Bridge* and *Beverly Hills 90210*, that they also have seen many more incidents of kindness?

> *"From* **Little House on the Prairie** *to* **The Golden Girls** *there is no end of people discovering their love for one another."*

From *Little House on the Prairie* to *The Golden Girls* there is no end of people discovering their love for one another. Singles, marrieds, siblings, punks and homeboys share so much peace, tolerance and understanding that you might even call it gratuitous harmony.

It is tempting to conclude that a young person bombarded with hours of dramas in which characters are good-hearted becomes more sensitized to niceness. The conclusion might be wrong, but it's just as plausible as arguing that TV encourages evil.

The "Dangers" of Radio, Storytelling

These issues have been around longer than television has, of course. In the 1930's and 40's, studies warned of the harmful effects radio was having on children's school performance and their ability to distinguish fantasy from reality. "This new invader of the privacy of the home has brought many a disturbing influence in its wake," a psychologist wrote in 1936. "Parents have become aware of a puzzling change in the behavior of their children."

Socrates cautioned that writing would destroy people's memories. Plato's *Republic* warned about the danger of storytellers: "Children cannot distinguish between what is allegory and what isn't, and opinions formed at that age are difficult to change." Comic books were once blamed for young people's poor reading ability, and the early days of film prompted books like *Movies, Delinquency, and Crime*.

Today, of course, we lament that no one writes anymore. And whatever happened to those old-time storytellers? Comic books? Films? Those comics and films are classics now. And it's a shame many of us weren't around to hear those wonderful shoot-'em-up *Gangbusters* in the golden days of radio.

It is possible that today's kids will survive the effects of new technology as well as earlier generations did—provided they aren't forced to watch panel discussions by the TV experts.

Chapter 2

Should Media Violence Be Censored?

CURRENT CONTROVERSIES

Chapter Preface

Almost 80 percent of Americans polled by the *Los Angeles Times* in 1993 expressed their belief that there is a connection between media violence and societal violence. Of those polled, more than half—54 percent—supported government guidelines to limit media violence.

But to many people, "government guidelines" is simply a euphemistic term for censorship, a word that conjures up images of zealots burning books or smashing record albums. This image and the thought of censoring violence in the media frighten many Americans. As columnist Carl Rowan writes, "Orgies of censorship, like all oppression movements, tend to take on a mindless life of their own." Rowan and others fear that censoring violence in the media could be the first step to government control of all speech, and could ultimately threaten all forms of communication.

Supporters of government regulation, however, believe it should be welcomed, not feared. Many of them applauded the actions of U.S. attorney general Janet Reno, who in 1993 stated that if media executives did nothing to reduce violence, she would impose government regulations. Columnist Neal Peirce reflected the views of many Reno supporters: "Reno is right. The entertainers will stall forever without threats. And it *is* quite reasonable to assume that thousands of murders, beatings, assaults in this nation would not have taken place if young people's minds had not been shaped and misshaped by the murderous violence which Hollywood has drummed into their consciences from infancy on."

Peirce, Reno, and others fear the effect media violence has on society. But censorship can also threaten a free society. The following chapter examines both the benefits and the hazards of censoring media violence.

Media Violence Should Be Censored

by Irving Kristol

About the author: *Irving Kristol, a fellow at the American Enterprise Institute, coedits the* Public Interest *and publishes the* National Interest.

On March 31, 1994, Britain experienced an unexpected cultural shock. That was when Professor Elizabeth Newson, head of the child development unit at Nottingham University, issued a report on violence-rich videos (known in the U.K. as "video nasties") and their effect on children. The report was signed by 25 psychologists and pediatricians, all known to be of the liberal persuasion. Its gist is summed up by the following quotations:

"Many of us hold our liberal ideals of freedom of expression dear, but now begin to feel that we were naive in our failure to predict the extent of damaging material and its all-too-free availability to children."

It then went on: "By restricting such material from home viewing, society must take on a necessary responsibility in protecting children from this, as from other forms of child abuse."

A storm of controversy ensued, which the American press largely ignored. A Labor member of Parliament introduced legislation to limit the availability of such "video nasties." The movie industry was naturally outraged, since so much of their profits come from the subsequent sale of videotapes, and they cried "Censorship!"—which, of course, is what was being advocated. More surprising was the reaction of the Tory Home Minister, Michael Howard, who turned out to be "wet" (we would say "soft") on this whole issue. He was very worried about all those households without children, whose freedom to watch "video nasties" would be circumscribed.

Both True and False

And then, inevitably, there were the unreconstructed liberal academics, who kept insisting that no one had ever proved a causal relation between TV violence and aggressive behavior by the young. This was both true and false. It was true in the sense that such clear-cut, causal relations are beyond the reach of social science—there are simply too many other factors that influence youthful behavior. It was false because there is an abundance of circumstantial evidence that points to the existence of such a relation—circumstantial evidence so strong as to raise no reasonable doubt in the minds of ordinary people, and of parents especially.

> *"Modest limits on adult liberties ought to be perfectly acceptable."*

In the Spring 1993 issue of *The Public Interest*, Brandon Centerwall, a professor of epidemiology at the University of Washington in Seattle, summarizes much of this circumstantial evidence. He focuses on research findings on the effect of television when it was introduced to rural, isolated communities in Canada and when English-language TV came to South Africa in 1975, having previously been banned by the Afrikaans-speaking government. In all such instances there was a spectacular increase in violent crime, most especially among the young.

Professor Centerwall also notes that when TV was introduced in the United States after World War II, the homicide rate among whites, who were the first to buy sets, began to rise, while the black homicide rate didn't show any such increase until four years later.

Statistical studies of the relation between youthful aggressiveness and TV can be deceptive, Professor Centerwall explains, if they focus on the overall, average response—which, indeed, seems weak. But aggressive impulses, like most human phenomena, are distributed along a bell-shaped curve, and it is at the margin where the significant effect is to be observed: "It is an intrinsic property of such 'bell curve' distributions that small changes in the average imply major changes at the extremes. Thus, if an exposure to television causes 8% of the population to shift from below-average aggression to above-average aggression, it follows that the homicide rate will double."

Professor Centerwall concludes that "the evidence indicates that if, hypothetically, television technology had never been developed, there would today be 10,000 fewer homicides each year in the United States, 70,000 fewer rapes, and 700,000 fewer injurious assaults. Violent crime would be half what it is."

Focus on the Children

So the evidence for some kind of controls over television (and tapes) is strong enough to provoke popular and political concern. It is certainly true that any such controls will involve some limitations on the freedom of adults to enjoy the kind of entertainment they might prefer. But modest limits on adult liberties ought to be perfectly acceptable if they prevent tens of thousands of our children from growing up into criminal adults. And it is the children we should be focusing on. The violence-prone adults, especially at the pathological fringe, are beyond our reach and, in most cases, beyond all possibility of redemption. It is the young people—especially those who have not yet reached adolescence—who are most affected by television, as all the studies agree.

Something will surely be done about this problem, despite the American Civil Liberties Union and other extreme interpreters of the First Amendment. In Britain, Mr. Howard reluctantly agreed to propose appropriate legislation, propelled by a powerful consensus among Tories, the Labor Party, the Liberal Party, the media and popular opinion. There is little doubt that, in the United States, a momentum for similar action is building up. How politicians will respond to it remains to be seen. But the idea that our popular culture can have malignant effects upon our young, and upon our society in its entirety, seems to be an idea whose coming cannot be long delayed.

And if there is a connection between our popular culture and the plague of criminal violence we are suffering from, then is it not reasonable to think that there may also be such a connection between our popular culture and the plagues of sexual promiscuity among teenagers, teenage illegitimacy, and, yes, the increasing number of rapes committed by teenagers? Here again, we don't really need social science to confirm what common sense and common observations tell us to be the case.

Can anyone really believe that soft porn in our Hollywood movies, hard porn in our cable movies, and violent porn in our "rap" music is without effect? Here, the average, overall impact is quite discernible to the naked eye. And at the margin, the effects, in terms most notably of illegitimacy and rape, are shockingly visible.

> *"True, censorship makes a difference only at the margin. But . . . it is at the margin where the crucial action is."*

Clearly, something must be done to lower the temperature of the sexual climate in which we live. And whatever is done, it will of necessity limit the freedoms of adults to indulge their sexual fantasies. Most of us will not mourn the loss of such freedoms, but—as with violence—there are those who will loudly protest any such rude "violation" of our "civil liberties."

Censorship, we will be told, is immoral—though no moral code of any society that has ever existed has ever deemed it so. Besides, we will be told further, it is ineffectual. Well, those of us who have lived in a slightly chillier sexual climate have survived as witnesses to the fact that it is not so ineffectual after all. True, censorship makes a difference only at the margin. But, and this cannot be repeated too often, it is at the margin where the crucial action is. This is as true for sexual activity as it is for economic activity.

An Invitation to Promiscuity

The most common (hypocritical and politically cowardly) response to the problems generated by our overheated sexual climate is that these are something parents have to do something about. But parents cannot do it on their own. They never have been able to do it on their own. Parents have always relied on churches, schools and the popular culture for help. Today, no such reliance is possible.

The mainline churches, still intoxicated with a vulgarized Freudianism, have discovered that sex is good and repression is bad. The schools hand out condoms to adolescents while timidly suggesting that they ought to limit their activity to "responsible sex." This is nothing less than an official invitation to promiscuity. The culture, meanwhile, is busy making as much money as possible out of as much sex as possible.

No, the government, at various levels, will have to step in to help the parents. And it will do so despite the anticipated cries of outrage from libertarians, liberal or conservative. The question, and it is no easy question, is just how to intervene. That is the issue that is now up for serious discussion.

Censoring Media Violence Is Necessary to Protect Children

by *American Medical News*

About the author: American Medical News *is the weekly newspaper of the American Medical Association.*

Television is pervasive and powerful.

Children are great imitators.

Why make two such statements in the same editorial?

What children see, they imitate. And what they see a lot of on both broadcast and cable TV, as well as in the movies, is violence both real and fake.

It's been estimated that a typical young person watches television 27 hours a week—some much more. By age 18, she or he will have seen 40,000 killings and 200,000 acts of violence.

A kid is bound to be affected by all that mayhem. Your grandmother could tell you that. But if common sense isn't enough, then science should suffice. Countless studies and expert panels have identified a clear link between aggressive behavior and violent programming.

Defenders of TV violence deny both science and sense. Perhaps the producers and programmers of television programming are so accustomed to living in their electronic neverland that they can't recognize reality when they see it. Or maybe it's the real-life profits that come from violent programming that makes them so reluctant to face the truth.

Violence Is Easy

In the TV industry, violent programming shares some of the same qualities of a Saturday night special—it's cheap and effective. Violent programming is a proven audience getter, easy to write and inexpensive to produce. Children are exposed to violence on programs that range from cartoons to the new breed of "reality" shows, like those about law enforcement.

In rejecting reasonable controls on the televised violence, the creators of violent programs invariably play their strongest defense—the freedom of speech card.

As a newspaper, we're especially sensitive to First Amendment arguments, but in this case it just doesn't wash.

"There's no such thing as a little censorship," lectured one industry insider to a recent conference on TV violence. But censorship and limits have always been an accepted part of television—especially on broadcast TV—and there's been nothing little about it. Even the most violent shows on broadcast TV still can't use some of the words that routinely pepper schoolyard banter, nor show nudity that mirrors images tame enough for the walls of the local art museum. What they have been given a pass on, until now, is violence. Cable TV, because it has greater latitude in what it can present, has raised the stakes even higher.

The movement to curb violent TV is less an attempt to curtail television's First Amendment rights than to cut the access of younger viewers, who clearly should not be exposed to it.

The pressure that's been building on this issue for some time may have begun to do some good. Increased attention, including congressional hearings, has prompted the major broadcast and top cable networks to promise warnings before their most violent shows. That's a welcome but very small step.

> *"As a newspaper, we're especially sensitive to First Amendment arguments, but in this case it just doesn't wash."*

The American Medical Association (AMA) has intensified its advocacy efforts, building on a history of opposition to TV violence dating from the mid-1970s.

The Association has endorsed a bill calling for new television sets to be equipped with a microprocessor—the so-called V-chip—that would allow households to screen out violent programs. It has also called on advertisers to pull their ads from violent shows.

In cooperation with a petition campaign by Senator Kent Conrad (D, N.D.) and his National Task Force on TV Violence, the AMA and other organizations have called on the Federal Communications Commission to hold hearings on television violence. The groups advocate guidelines and a violence rating system for programming during prime time and children's viewing hours. The standards would be enforced through fines and threat of license revocation. The petitions will be presented to the FCC, along with broadcast and cable TV leaders and the Motion Picture Association of America.

Video Games Should Be Censored

by Lionel Van Deerlin

About the author: *Lionel Van Deerlin was a California representative in Congress for eighteen years.*

Have you played a video game called Night Trap? With a hand-held control, you try to defend a group of sorority girls in scanty pajamas against a horde of blood-sucking intruders.

For someone who never even went along on a panty raid, this is heady stuff. The game makes a technological leap ahead of the familiar Nintendo offerings of past seasons, in that Night Trap's characters are real-live actors, not the computer-generated figures of earlier games.

But if blood-sucking is not your thing, plenty of other new video software may brighten your day, at $20 to as much as $60 per purchase. In a street-fighting game called Mortal Kombat, the skilled player can pluck out the spinal column of an on-screen victim.

Another, labeled Lethal Enforcer, reflects tellingly on our society of armed households. Instead of the conventional control device, participants acquire an electronically charged handgun (a "justifier," in the game's glossary) for firing point-blank into the TV screen—and, with good aim, for taking out the bad guys.

"You won't find toys like this in any Crackerjack box," says an ad for Lethal Enforcer.

Stanching the Gore

Well, let's hope not. Let's hope, too, that some reasonable regulation—by government, if the game manufacturers themselves cannot come to terms with public decency—will stanch this video gore.

Warnings have come from widely divergent sources—from a Senate subcommittee chaired by liberal Democrat Joseph Lieberman of Connecticut, and from California's conservative Republican attorney general, Dan Lungren.

Lionel Van Deerlin, "The Electronic Slaughter of the Innocents," *San Diego Union*, December 21, 1993. Reprinted with permission.

"Lieberman has threatened government action if the electronic games industry fails to temper violence and rampant sex in a product aimed mainly at children." Lungren wants certain games withdrawn from sales shelves forthwith.

A Predictable Reaction

Industry reaction was predictable. Commercial success often breeds arrogance—highlighted in this instance by one Thomas Zito, president of Digital Pictures Inc., the producer of Night Trap. Zito sees his business as all fun and games, without a hint of social significance.

"It's preposterous to claim there is a causal relationship between a video game and anyone getting a bullet in the back," this captain of industry told Lieberman's Senate oversight committee.

So here we have someone practicing child psychology without a license. Zito's testimony airily dismisses most academic opinion regarding the rise in violence among school kids.

In an effort to head off a government crackdown, however, the producers of video games have promised a modicum of reform. Unfortunately, this effort was directed not to content of the gory games themselves, only to their marketing. The manufacturers said they'll provide a "rating system" warning buyers as to the degree of each product's predilection to violence.

Is this to be taken seriously? One of the first companies to adopt a rating system was Sega of America.

"Let's hope, too, that some reasonable regulation—by government . . . —will stanch this video gore."

This is the firm whose prize package is Mortal Kombat, in which aggressors rip off people's heads amid realistic spurts of blood—preceding the aforementioned *coup de grâce* of a lost spinal column.

Sega's vice president for marketing, William White Jr., conceded to senators that such mayhem may be inappropriate for tots. In a burst of corporate responsibility, Sega assigned Mortal Kombat an "MA-13" rating to indicate its ultimate violence and supposedly to invite parental discretion in what they buy.

Loopholes and Hypocrisy

But Mortal Kombat, like most of these games, can be found in countless video arcades—in hotels, shopping malls and fun areas where it is available to any kid with quarters in his jeans. No warning label and no questions asked. Any rating system with which this industry seeks to head off government action is so fraught with loopholes (to say nothing of hypocrisy) as to fool no one.

Voluntary regulation? Nintendo of America estimates it lost $10 million by toning down its own version of Mortal Kombat. How long will stockholders permit this out-of-pocket display of concern for America's children?

Congress has shown considerable patience toward an industry whose social conscience comes with batteries not included. The reluctance to impose content standards is commendable. Government never performs satisfactorily as a censor, and should not be encouraged to try.

Yet this is no First Amendment matter, either. If the video game outrage compels rule-making, it should not be equated with the anathema of press or broadcasting censorship. We feel no hesitancy in going after the marketers of toys which can cut, strangle or otherwise threaten children physically. Is it not irresponsible to permit the poisoning of young *minds*?

Media Violence Should Not Be Censored

by Robert Scheer

About the author: *Robert Scheer is an author and a contributing editor for the* Los Angeles Times.

Once again Congressional committees are holding hearings on TV violence, and network executives, sincere visages firmly in place, are promising to clean up their act. Attorney General Janet Reno testified that if they don't, "government should respond."

Beside the Point

There is something so beside the point about this hand-wringing, which has gone on since 1952, when the first Congressional hearing on TV violence was held. In 1968 a national commission headed by Milton Eisenhower warned: "We are deeply troubled by the television's constant portrayal of violence . . . in pandering to a public preoccupation with violence that television itself has helped to generate."

Of course, violence and base stupidity on TV and in the movies is excessive and getting worse. With the proliferation of cable channels, the market has become much more competitive, and violence sells. Hardly a night of channel-flipping goes by when my cable service doesn't offer up several truly grotesque chainsaw massacre–type films complete with dismembered parts and spurting blood.

Then, too, there are the cleaner assassinations presented on the networks both in their entertainment and local news hours. Remember the orgy of voyeurism, with three separate network movies devoted to the Amy Fisher–Joey Buttafuoco story? So-called news shows featuring real-life crime represent a major segment of entertainment scheduling. The fatal graveside shooting of a woman by her ex-spouse, captured by a television news camera, was gratuitously "teased" during the evening in many markets to get people to watch the news that night.

Robert Scheer, "Violence Is Us," *The Nation*, November 15, 1993. Reprinted with permission from *The Nation* magazine, © The Nation Company, L.P.

Nor do I deny the claims of most experts that viewing violence desensitizes people, particularly children, to the actual effects of violence, leaving them more likely to act out in antisocial ways. As the American Psychological Association reported to Congress in 1988, "Virtually all independent scholars agree that there is evidence that television can cause aggressive behavior."

More than 200 major studies support the common-sense suspicion that watching endless hours of violence is a public health menace. Those same studies demonstrate, although the pro-censorship prudes will never accept it, that the violent R-rated movies—not the sexually explicit X-rated ones—desensitize men to sexual violence. (As an example of this weirdly skewed double standard, wannabe censor Rev. Donald Wildmon took out full-page ads attacking *NYPD Blue*, not for for its explicit violence—six homicides in the first episode—but rather because of a nude lovemaking scene, calling it "soft-core pornography.")

Poverty, Children, and Guns

Another thing those studies show is that the poorer a family is, meaning the more vulnerable and desperate, the more hours they will spend in front of the television set. Children in poverty are most often left alone with the TV as the only available babysitter.

It can hardly be a good thing that children's shows in 1991 reached an all-time high of thirty-two violent incidents per hour and that nine in ten children's programs involve violence. An authoritative study by George Gerbner of the University of Pennsylvania indicated that the average 16-year-old has witnessed 200,000 violent acts on TV, including 33,000 murders. Given the ease with which children can get guns in this society, there has to be some connection between the ease with which citizens are blown away by teenagers on television and in what passes for real life. And when they do it in real life they can be assured of their fifteen minutes of fame with top billing on the nightly local news.

Wayne LaPierre, vice president of the National Rifle Association, had a good point when he complained, "It galls us that every night we get lectured by ABC, NBC and CBS News, and then they go to their entertainment programming and show all kinds of gratuitous violence." Hypocrites they are, and the voluntary labeling code that the network executives adopted in an effort to head off Congressional prohibitions on violent programming will change nothing. Although 72

> *"It is time to face the fact that we have all this mayhem in our art and our lives because we like violence."*

percent of Americans polled by Times-Mirror say that we have too much violence on TV and it leads to higher crime rates, many of them must be tuning in, or the television moguls wouldn't be scheduling such fare.

Maybe it is time to face the fact that we have all this mayhem in our art and our lives because we like violence. Or if we don't actually like it, we need it.

Why else would we favor local news programs that stress ambulance-chasing "action news"? Whether it's local or foreign news, our attention is grabbed completely only when death and destruction are at hand. That's what the endless focus groups conducted by news organizations report. It is true, as Steven Bochco, creator of *NYPD Blue*, has stated, that the violence issue on prime time is a "bogus issue," because "there's more violence on the 5 o'clock news than anything you'll see on the networks during prime time."

Children's Needs, Adults' Wishes

Anyway, how can you control it without putting decision-making into the hands of small-minded censors? What are the guidelines? Some reasonable ones, to cut the harmful effects on children, were suggested by University of Michigan psychology professor Leonard Eron, who is the dean of research in this area. "Gratuitous violence that is not necessary to the plot should be reduced or eliminated" is one that the networks say they accept. Another we can all agree on is that the "devastating effects of violence, the permanence of its consequences . . . should be made clear," meaning you hurt or die from gunshot wounds. So far so good, but what about when he tells us, "Perpetrators of violence should not be rewarded for their violent acts," and that "those who act aggressively should be punished"? Those last two, while admirable goals, would distort a reality in which many criminals do get away with their crimes. Do we want television writers to lie to us? Don't we adults need to face up to the truth that crime is out of control?

> *"It is absurd to suggest that the government step in to censor viewing."*

Maybe adults should watch what they want, but should children, who are by definition impressionable, be exposed to a steady diet of mind-numbing violence laced with general stupidity? No, they shouldn't, but is this an issue the government or other would-be censors ought to get involved with?

The answer is, They are already involved, but despite endless guidelines for children's television, the fare is nastier than ever. The reason is that every regulation produces just that much more ingenuity on the part of the so-called creative people who make this junk. They are a crafty bunch and will always find some way of getting to the kids with the most primitive jolt.

Take the much-discussed *Beavis and Butt-Head* show, which now leads the race for the lowest common denominator. When a 5-year-old in Ohio burned the family trailer to the ground, his mother blamed the show, her son's favorite, which had shown the two idiot characters setting fire to all sorts of objects. Hey, no problem, arson was taken out of the show in response to public outrage. There were the expected calls to ban *Beavis*, but no one stopped to ask the obvious question: Why had that mother let her 5-year-old watch endless hours of this repulsive show?

I asked the same question after reading a story in the *Los Angeles Times* about firefighters having to visit the schools of Orange County, California, to warn the kids that setting fires at home is a no-no. In one class, almost all the 12-year-olds said they watched *Beavis and Butt-Head* regularly and then began chanting the call of the show's lead, "Burn, burn, burn." That was in the conservative white upper-middle-class community of Mission Viejo, one of those planned paradises. Again, why did all those parents allow their kids to watch the show? It is absurd to suggest that the government step in to censor viewing that parents have acquiesced in.

Dismissing the Impact of Media Violence

The more important question is, Why do the children of paradise delight in this and other stupidities? I don't really know the full answer but it can't be, as Dan Quayle charged in the 1992 election, that the cultural elite of Hollywood has seized their minds. Orange County voted overwhelmingly for Quayle and his running mate, the parents have thrown up the strongest defenses against Satan and his permissiveness, and church, Little League and Boy Scout attendance is very high.

One answer provided by the creators of this stuff is that it doesn't mean a thing. Kids have always tuned in to cartoons and movies in which characters are splattered or blown away. They concede that things are a bit wilder now, with far more blood and gore and nastier images, but that's modern technology for you. The demand is there and the supply will follow, but no harm is done— it's just a picture.

I don't buy this argument, because the impact of television and movies is too pervasive to be so easily dismissed. For many kids the electronic picture is their world, the result of an ever more technically effective medium having drowned out all other avenues of learning and stimulation.

It does desensitize and, yes, I don't think young kids should be watching *Beavis and Butt-Head* scenes featuring a poke in the eye with a pencil with blood spurting out, or a dog thrown into a washing machine followed by an insane giggle of approval. I doubt very much that *Beavis* creator Mike Judge will allow his little girls to watch the show.

> *"Trying to ban something just makes it more attractive and marketable."*

But "we," collectively, can't and should not do anything about it. We can't because we live in a market economy in which blood lust and other primitive needs of people will be met one way or another, and trying to ban something just makes it more attractive and marketable. We shouldn't because it is the adults' right to flick on whatever they want on the increasingly responsive cable smorgasbord. And it is parents' responsibility to monitor what kids watch. The "we" as represented by the state should do nothing.

The alternative is for the public, or rather some segment of it, to demand something better on at least a few of the many channels that are opening up. There are plenty of good television programs and movies that aim higher and do well at the box office. Since the market is master, people need not be passive about expressing their tastes. Where I live, for example, people have demanded successfully that the cable company carry the excellent Bravo channel, which it was threatening to drop.

The Advertisers Are Key

"In the final analysis, it is still the law of supply and demand on all this stuff," says Norman Lear, whose *All in the Family* series first upped the ante for thoughtful prime-time programming.

> It goes back to the advertisers; they are the people who pay for this stuff. If they didn't want it, it wouldn't be there. They are just dealing with product. They know from experience that something hard and outrageous will sell faster than something soft.

> It's no secret that there's a lot of baseness to human nature, but we don't always pander to it, and reasonable people don't wish to pander to it. But there is nothing reasonable about the bottom line and about needing to please Wall Street by the quarter—to find the instant rating successes that satisfy the bottom line.

> The network goes to someone to make a pilot, then they take it to Madison Avenue, and people look at it and say, "That's a fucking hit!" They're the first people to look at it and say, "I want in. I will spend my millions of dollars here because I think it will rate."

He adds that because no single sponsor is identified with a show, as was the case in the "Golden Age" of the *Philco Playhouse* and the *Alcoa Hour*, "no sponsor is seriously associated with the quality of the show."

"It is the adults' right to flick on whatever they want."

That's what happened with *Beavis and Butt-Head*—its creator, Judge, had originally prepared it as a one-time entry for a festival of "sick and twisted" cartoons. He had no intention of turning his one-liner into a series, but MTV execs saw it and ordered up thirty-five episodes, and soon it was a multinational operation with teams of animators in New York and Korea frantically turning the stuff out.

The MTV execs were right. The demand was there. It's MTV's hottest show, and more episodes are on the way for worldwide distribution. If you don't like that because you think it represents the dumbing-down of American and world culture, then vote—by just turning the damn thing off. Don't beg Big Brother to do it for you.

Censoring Media Violence Would Be Ineffective

by Stephen Chapman

About the author: *Stephen Chapman is a regular columnist for* Human Events, *a conservative weekly newspaper.*

The existence of a problem does not mean there is a solution. But politicians are not given to stoic acceptance of social imperfections, which they believe can be overcome by robust applications of government power.

Congress is considering several measures to curb violence on television, an annoyance that has been inflated into a crisis so that politicians can let their consciences be our guide.

The assumption behind the proposals circulating on Capitol Hill is almost universally accepted: A society cannot subsist on an endless diet of televised violence without becoming unbearably violent itself. Kids who spend hours watching people do physical harm to one another, the theory goes, will grow up to do likewise. TV is violent; our society is violent and has grown more so since the rise of TV; therefore, it must be TV that makes us violent.

A Gory and Placid Society

But we know that a society can be soaked in glamorized gore and be as placid as the prairies.

Consider Canada, most of which has daily access to our programs and which remains stolidly resistant to the charms of violence. The United States has 9 times as many people as Canada but 36 times as many homicides. A lot of countries have imported our TV series, few of them our crime rate.

Nor does American lawlessness have any obvious connection to what goes out over the airwaves. The 1980s were only slightly more murderous than the 1930s, before TV could be blamed. The national habit of violence is not a recent creation of Steven Bochco.

No one seems to have noticed that broadcast television has gotten less bloody

Stephen Chapman, "Censorship Won't Eliminate Violent Crime," *Human Events*, October 16, 1993. Reprinted by permission of Stephen Chapman and Creators Syndicate.

in recent years, not more.

Jack Valenti, head of the Motion Picture Association of America, said in a July 1993 speech that "the 25 most popular series, most of which are situation comedies, have no violence." Police dramas, which used to be common, are now rare. Those who hoped to see a pacifying effect from this trend, though, have been disappointed.

Violence on TV may be no more to blame for crime in the streets than Judy Blume is for teen-age pregnancies—even a well-known critic like University of Washington epidemiologist Brandon Centerwall estimates that watching TV makes kids only 5% more aggressive. But politicians hate to miss any chance to appease popular discontent.

"I can tell you that none of the sponsors of these initiatives is losing votes back home with these ideas," acknowledges Illinois Senator Paul Simon (D.). In the tradition of those Oklahomans who, it was said, would regularly stagger to the polls to vote dry, the public dislikes TV violence so much it can barely stand to keep the set on.

Separating Good Violence from Bad

There are several ideas percolating on Capitol Hill. Simon has asked the industry to take remedial action, while thoughtfully advising that if it doesn't, Congress will. The threat was enough to persuade the networks to start running parental advisories on graphic shows.

Representative Edward Markey, the Massachusetts Democrat who chaired the telecommunications subcommittee, proposed requiring TV makers to install a chip that would let owners block any show carrying a code signaling violent content.

Senator Ernest Hollings, South Carolina Democrat, wants to ban excessive violence except during the hours when most kids are in bed. Representative John Bryant, Texas Democrat, suggests that the Federal Communications Commission deny license renewals to stations that offend congressional standards.

But how do we separate good violence from bad violence? Presumably no one wants to regulate the content of local TV newscasts, some of which have made their living on the motto, "If it bleeds, it leads."

Nor is anyone brave enough to suggest that the National Football League or professional boxing be exiled to the middle of the night. And when

"A society can be soaked in glamorized gore and be as placid as the prairies."

PBS shows Shakespeare's King Lear gouging out his own eyes or Henry V piling up French corpses at Agincourt, the TV police will probably not object. Brutality is fine if it's newsworthy, athletic or highbrow.

Congress may be able to find ways to alter the composition of broadcast TV without running afoul of the First Amendment, though it isn't easy. But the most gruesome fare is on cable and video, where the Supreme Court is no more likely to tolerate federal interference with content than it would in books and movies. So the value of forcing the networks to minimize mayhem is likely to be somewhere between tiny and zero.

That inconvenient fact aside, it would be a mistake to let the government expand its role in deciding what Americans should be allowed to see and hear of their own free will. Maybe some TV researcher could put aside the question of whether TV induces us to commit violence and investigate whether it causes us to demand that the government run our lives.

Censorship of Media Violence Threatens Freedom of Speech

by Virginia I. Postrel

About the author: *Virginia I. Postrel is the editor of* Reason, *a magazine of political and social opinion.*

When the Chicago Bulls won their third world championship, riots broke out in Chicago, killing three people. When the Montreal Canadiens took the Stanley Cup, the ensuing riots injured 168 and did $10 million in damage. The Dallas Cowboys' Super Bowl victory produced similar results.

You do not have to be a social scientist to see the relation. Sports championships cause violence.

But calling for an end to the Super Bowl or the National Basketball Association championship games will not win politicians the applause of journalists and social critics. Dragging Michael Jordan in front of a Senate committee and demanding that he justify his profession will not make Senator Paul Simon any friends back home in Illinois.

Denouncing television violence will. From Senator Estes Kefauver in the 1950s on, politicians with a love for the nanny state and an instinct for the spotlight have decried TV violence to attract the cameras to themselves.

Critics' Proposals

The networks' agreement to put warning labels on particularly violent shows will not end the calls for censorship. Senator Byron Dorgan (D-N.D.) says the warnings are "like having a chemical company paint their smokestack red to say here's where the pollution is being emitted." Pat Buchanan says the First Amendment doesn't protect "cultural pollution." And Michigan gadfly Terry Rakolta still wants the Federal Communications Commission to ban "violent" programming from 4 p.m. to 9 p.m. Interim FCC Chairman Jim Quello sup-

Virginia I. Postrel, "TV Violence Rouses the Old Itch to Censor," *Los Angeles Times*, July 8, 1993.
Reprinted with permission. Copyright 1993 by the Reason Foundation, 3415 S. Sepulveda Blvd., Suite 400, Los Angeles, CA 90034. (310) 391-2245.

ported her proposal.

The "problem" of TV violence is not a problem of uninformed viewers. People did not tune in *Murder in the Heartland* expecting *Little House on the Prairie*. Roseanne hasn't suddenly started taking a hatchet to her sit-com kids. The problem, in the minds of critics, is that television violence exists at all.

That is why the critics are never satisfied. If TV violence is realistic, as in reality cop shows, they complain that it leads people to think the world is threatening. If it is unrealistic, as in cartoons, they complain that

> *"Politicians . . . have decried TV violence to attract the cameras to themselves."*

it is desensitizing. If violence is portrayed as painful or bloody, they complain about gore. If it is portrayed as clean, they complain about trivialization.

They disdain both the nihilistic *Murder in the Heartland* and the moral *Wiseguy*. If villains use violence to hurt people, critics gripe about bad role models. If heroes use violence to save people, they're teaching that violence solves problems, critics say.

If broadcasters propose a warning for parents that a show may be inappropriate for children, critics say the parents may not be around. If parents are around, what about kids who have their own TV sets in their bedrooms? And if a family has no TV at all, what about kids watching violent shows at friends' houses?

These are not arguments for more parental information. They are arguments for banning art. And we have heard them before.

Comics and Censorship

Back in the 1950s, when Kefauver, a Tennessee Democrat and vice-presidential aspirant, was not crusading against television, he was crusading against comic books. Inspired by Dr. Fredric Wertham's 1953 book, *Seduction of the Innocent* (now a touchstone example of overwrought Eisenhower-era fears of sex, violence and social deviance), Kefauver held hearings to bully the comic book industry into "doing something" about the problem of crime comics and comics-inspired juvenile delinquency. Comics, it was argued, were uniquely pervasive and uncontrollable by parents.

In response, the industry created the Comics Code, wiping out all adult comics. For the next two decades, comic books were utterly banal. An entire genre, the serous graphic novel, was destroyed, the good with the bad. In the name of children, and a small minority of violent children at that, the freedom of nonviolent adults to read, write, draw and publish was obliterated.

That is what the critics of television violence are driving toward. Some, like the National Coalition on Television Violence, are ideological pacifists. Some, like Buchanan or Michael Medved, are conservatives at war with popular culture. Some, like Rakolta, are meddlesome moms. Some watch television; most do not.

Chapter 2

Their motives and ideologies are different. But all seek to use the official violence of government power to wipe out ideas and images they do not like. They say those ideas and images inspire crimes. So do love and hate, religion and politics. So, even, do national basketball championships.

But in a free society we distinguish between ideas and actions. And we do not sacrifice the artistic and commercial freedom of the many to the violent acts— or political posturing—of the few.

Chapter 3

Can the Media Effectively Regulate Violence in Their Products?

CURRENT CONTROVERSIES

The Media and Violence: An Overview

by Harrison Rainie, Betsy Streisand, and Monika Guttman with Gordon Witkin

About the authors: *Harrison Rainie, Betsy Streisand, Monika Guttman, and Gordon Witkin are staff members of* U.S. News & World Report.

And now, from the folks who brought you three versions of the Amy Fisher–Joey Buttafuoco story, quickie movies on the David Koresh shootout and the World Trade Center bombing, bizarre brutality in *Wild Palms* and infanticide in *Murder in the Heartland*, comes this startling concept: "Due to some violent content, parental discretion advised." The explicit warning adopted by ABC, CBS, NBC and Fox network executives is new, but it arises from a fear that has gnawed at Americans since the first days when Robert Stack, playing Eliot Ness, shot it up with gangsters every week in *The Untouchables* in the 1950s. As the (Milton) Eisenhower Commission put it in 1969: "We are deeply troubled by the television's constant portrayal of violence . . . in pandering to a public preoccupation with violence that television itself has helped to generate."

Shortcomings

The problem is that the warning system won't cover much of the mayhem on the tube. Only one regular-season show, Steven Bochco's *NYPD Blue*, will contain the warning—and that was decided *before* the networks [adopted the warning]. Presumably, the warning will also be slapped on a handful of movies. But it will not be applied to: cable station offerings, which in "adult" programming have an even bloodier tinge than network shows; independently produced shows like the new *Untouchables*; children's TV shows, which in the 1990–91 network season reached a historically high 32 violent acts per hour during network weekend TV; any newscasts, including local TV news, which in many cities has become a near ceaseless chronicle of gore; and reality-based TV shows like *Cops*.

Another shortcoming is that each network will decide for itself when to issue an advisory. There will be no uniform standard for what constitutes worrisome violence. "The advisories will have absolutely no effect," predicts David Abbott, director of the Boston-based Foundation to Improve Television, an antiviolence advocacy group.

Happy Violence

There has been a long-running debate about whether this saturation of media violence, including the routine barbarity in movies, video games and comic books, is causally connected to the actual level of violence in modern culture. Whatever the linkage, there is now widespread agreement that the public understanding of violence—especially that of children—has been recast over time. "The historically limited, individually crafted, selectively used and often tragic symbolic violence [of fairy tales, myths and Shakespeare] has been swamped by 'happy violence,'" argues critic George Gerbner. "Happy violence shows no pain or tragic consequences. It is a swift and easy dramatic solution to many problems."

Whatever the scientific truth, there has been a surprising convergence of opinion that media violence abets the real violence on America's streets. The urgency of the current debate began after the trauma of the 1992 Los Angeles riots as then Vice President Quayle and others attacked Hollywood for its loose morals. It was fueled by an especially bloodthirsty run of made-for-TV movies that aired during ratings "sweeps" periods. The May one, in particular, was called "one of the bloodiest months in TV history," by North Dakota Sen. Kent Conrad because 18 of the 29 network movie slots were filled with films or miniseries containing significant levels of violence. Not surprisingly, Congress is getting into the act, threatening everything from warning-label standards to requirements that new TVs include technology that allows parents to block out certain shows.

Turned Off

Driving the fervor is the increasingly assertive concern among parents of all persuasions who fear most that their kids will be warped or frightened by it all. But adults also embrace larger purposes. Liberals have drifted to the cause on the theory that better, more positive media images can lead to social improvement. Conservatives,

> *"Happy violence shows no pain or tragic consequences."*

who have been in the trenches longer, are especially anxious to press their argument that Hollywood is run by a pack of brutality-loving libertines. Fully 96 percent of the 70,000 persons who recently responded to a write-in survey by *USA Weekend* said Hollywood executives glorify violence and an equal number said they had switched off a show before it ended because of its violence.

One especially intriguing alliance is helping galvanize the crusade—the budding cooperative work between gun advocates and gun controllers. The Center to Prevent Handgun Violence has set up a Hollywood office to press for a more realistic portrayal of the devastating consequences of gun violence—for example,

> *"There's more violence on the five o'clock news than anything you'll see on the networks during prime time."*

ple, that a gun victim can end up permanently paralyzed in a wheelchair. The National Rifle Association would like to see guns used more responsibly, as well. "It galls us that every night we get lectured by ABC, NBC and CBS News, and then they go to their entertainment programming and show all kinds of gratuitous violence," says NRA Executive Vice President Wayne LaPierre.

Hollywood's response has been a strange admixture. One ingredient is contrition. *Wild Palms*, the exotic miniseries produced by movie director Oliver Stone, for example, was so gruesome that just two days after it aired, CBS Broadcast Group President Howard Stringer found himself promising a Senate subcommittee, "Definitely, we're going to do better."

Another ingredient is defiance. "This is a bogus issue," says Bochco, creator of such groundbreaking shows as *Hill Street Blues*. "There's more violence on the 5 o'clock news than anything you'll see on the networks during prime time." During many weeks that's true. The nonviolent half-hour family sitcom remains the staple of network programming.

Hypocrisy

Of course, no media executive's reaction to public concern would be complete without a dose of hypocrisy. In a *mea culpa* before the House telecommunications subcommittee on June 25, 1993, Ted Turner, chairman of CNN and TBS, said TV executives who put violent programs on the air were "guilty of murder as far as I can see. They all are. Me, too." This worthy sentiment comes almost five months to the day after TBS ran this promotional ad a week before the Super Bowl: "No football? No problem. A day of unnecessary roughness, personal fouls and sudden death." The featured films included the standard ferocious fare of Chuck Norris, Jean-Claude Van Damme and Clint Eastwood.

Most intriguing of all Hollywood's responses have been attempts by some to make violence morally instructive. Eastwood said his Oscar-winning Western, *Unforgiven*, was designed to "preach that it isn't glamorous to take a gun; it isn't glamorous to kill people; it isn't pretty." (Yet his next film, *In the Line of Fire*, centered on a madman's attempt to assassinate the president.) Even more daring, perhaps, are the hopes of Albert and Allen Hughes, the 21-year-old twins from Detroit who created the most graphically brutal film of the season, *Menace II Society*. In that film, gunshot victims appear on the screen almost every 15 minutes. The victims are filmed convulsing, salivating and in every other dimension of agony. The reason, according to Allen: "We make *realistically* violent scenes that almost make people want to turn their heads when they see it. You bring [youths] in [the theater], you appall them, you make them sick from the violence." Agrees Albert: "That really messes with people."

Advertiser Fallout

In Hollywood, though, ethical issues usually fall victim to the bottom line. And these days, economic currents provide the most hope against purveyors of violence. ABC's made-for-TV movie *Murder in the Heartland* was so violent that advertisers deserted it in droves, costing the network several million dollars. NBC reportedly rejected two projects for the 1993–94 season—a sequel to its Koresh movie and a TV-showing of Michael Douglas's *Falling Down*—because of fear the violence may incite criticism. "This is an industry based on trends," says independent producer Jennifer Alward. "The networks are turning away from violence. The buzzword these days is 'family trauma stories with an edge.'"

Media Executives Work to Curb Violence

by Monika Guttman

About the author: *Monika Guttman is a reporter for* U.S. News & World Report, *a weekly newsmagazine.*

When the cameras rolled on ABC's miniseries adaptation of James Michener's *Texas*, one particular incident did not move from page to screen: a bloody moment from the era before Texas's statehood when 1,100 men were lined up and killed by bayonet. In 1993, says Executive Producer Aaron Spelling, the scene might have been shot. And in the production offices of ABC's *Lois & Clark* series, creators and writers huddled to find a benign way to illustrate gang violence in one episode. The solution: using a stun gun instead of bullets. Leslie Moonves, president of Warner Bros. Television, producer of *Lois & Clark*, sees a pattern here: "So much more of the violence is off-camera in all series and pilots."

A Sense of Responsibility

Welcome to Hollywood's mean streets, 1994. Since May 1993, when Congress summoned television executives to testify about TV violence, the entertainment industry has been pulling its punches. Marketing and ratings pressures have abetted the trend. But a path-breaking survey by *U.S. News & World Report* and the University of California at Los Angeles suggests that many top-level Hollywood figures feel a sense of responsibility about the influence violence in entertainment is having on American society. Some 59 percent of the respondents say they consider TV and movie violence a problem. Nearly 9 out of 10 say that it contributes to the level of violence plaguing the nation, and a surprising 63 percent say the entertainment media glorify violence. "This is clearly an issue of enormous importance to the entertainment industry," summarizes Jeffrey Cole, director of UCLA's Center for Communication Policy. "They feel under siege, beleaguered—and that they have some responsibility for the problem. But they also feel that they are singled out for blame more than other societal causes of violence."

Some of the views of the 867 Hollywood respondents—executives, directors, writers and actors—were in sync with public sentiment. In a general-opinion survey, *U.S. News* found that 79 percent of voters believe violence in television and movies is a problem, and 91 percent think media mayhem contributes to real-life violence. In response, a clear majority of Hollywood leaders say they are willing to take several voluntary steps to address the issue. But they part company with the public on how serious the media violence problem is—and on whether the government should have any role in attacking it.

How Hollywood Sees Its Faults

Entertainment industry leaders said in a U.S. News–UCLA *survey that their business suffered from problems on several fronts.*

Do you consider any of these to be serious problems in current television programming?

	Very Serious Problem	Somewhat of a Problem	Not Much of a Problem
Poor quality of the shows themselves	46%	36%	18%
Violence	37%	43%	20%
Racial stereotyping	30%	45%	24%
Gender stereotyping	28%	46%	26%
Sexually explicit scenes/dialogue	15%	25%	60%

Most Hollywood figures call 1993's congressional complaints a distraction. The great majority blame factors such as poverty, drugs and alcohol, poor schooling, lax gun control and a general breakdown of families—not screen violence—for what goes on in real life. Scholars who have studied the link between media violence and the real world tend to agree. "It is a cause, but not even a main cause," notes John Wright, co-director of the University of Kansas Center for Research on the Influences of TV on Children.

Still, a number of bills restricting TV violence are on Congress's

> *"Many top-level Hollywood figures feel a sense of responsibility about the influence violence in entertainment is having on American society."*

agenda. Fully 83 percent of Hollywood survey respondents say the debate has affected the industry. Just in the 1993–1994 year:

- Networks, studios, production companies and industry groups arranged meetings with violence experts to distribute information about the effects of violence in entertainment and to discuss alternative ways of portraying dramatic conflict. One such discussion came at Paramount Television, which produces TV shows like *Star Trek: Deep Space Nine* and *The Untouchables*, where television writers and producers met several times with the Reverend Ellwood Kieser of the respected Humanitas Prize Organization. The Entertainment Industries Council, which distributes suggestions for writers and producers on social issues like drug use and AIDS, is meeting with writers and producers to develop ways for dramatizing conflict without violence and for showing the consequences of violence.

• Children's programmers, saying they are under double fire because of Federal Communications Commission rules and the violence debate, are adding new educational programs to their fare. At the top-rated Fox Children's Network, the animated *Where on Earth Is Carmen Sandiego?* debuted in February 1994, and three educational live action/animated weekday shows are in production.

Where Hollywood Places the Blame

Entertainment leaders think other kinds of programs also pump too many violent images into American homes.

With respect to the content of television programming, rank the following based on your concern about violence:

	Significant Concern	Moderate Concern	Little Concern
Local newscasts	49%	31%	20%
Reality series	41%	35%	24%
Action dramas (police shows, movies, similar)	38%	40%	21%
Cartoons/children live action	30%	37%	33%
Promotional spots for news and other shows	28%	33%	39%
National newscasts	25%	43%	32%

• At MTV, nearly 1 out of 3 music videos submitted is being ruled inappropriate for broadcast, up from 1 in 4 in 1993. It's not that 1994's crop is more violent. "We're taking a harder look at them," concedes MTV President Judy McGrath.

• Network and cable companies have stepped up antiviolence messages, which include public service announcements, an NBC special, "Lives in Hazard," with Edward James Olmos, and "Enough Is Enough," a campaign on MTV that featured a forum on violence with President Clinton. CBS and Fox simultaneously broadcast "Kids Killing Kids," a special on guns

and children.
- The cable industry promised to eliminate the gratuitous portrayal of violence as "an easy and convenient solution to human problems."
- Network and cable groups have solicited proposals from independent monitoring groups to measure violent program content.
- The network TV lineup is likely to continue a decade-long trend away from violence-laced shows. Filmmaker Wes Craven says NBC loved his murder-mystery pilot, *Laurel Canyon*,

> *"Networks . . . arranged meetings with violence experts to distribute information about the effects of violence in entertainment."*

but dropped it quickly after the congressional hearings. "There are cop shows, but they're going to deal with more psychological aspects than violence," says Betsy Frank of Saatchi & Saatchi, which buys ad time for clients. Finally, there are uncountable stories coming out of Hollywood about plot changes being made to respond to public sensitivities, and they involve more than just violence. Frank notes that ABC has promised advertisers that the critically acclaimed *NYPD Blue* is "undergoing changes and will not be the same show they put on the air in 1993."

Some fear the industry has gone too far. "It has a chilling impact," argues NBC West Coast President Don Ohlmeyer. "Films that ought to be on TV, that might have an important message, won't be." Film director Oliver Stone agrees: "Films have become more sanitized. We're moving away from reality. We're in the grip of a political correctness that's bothersome." In fact, Stone's movie *Natural Born Killers* focuses on media glorification of violence.

Hard to Define Violence

For all the change, the industry has not made one harmonious leap toward clear-cut standards. One reason is that it's hard to define violence. Hollywood remains divided on exactly who is most culpable—film, entertainment TV or news. The *U.S. News*–UCLA survey turned up several points of tension:

• *Reality shows; local news.* A third of the respondents listed local TV news and "reality shows"—like Fox's *Cops*—as serious concerns in the violence debate. Producers for these shows say they, too, are changing. "Advertisers want to see scripts in advance more than in the past," notes Mike Hegedus, executive producer of the syndicated series *Prime Suspect*, which is based on real-life crimes. Hegedus, a journalist for 26 years, says reality shows have to subscribe to journalistic principles to be credible—and censorship of news "is a whole different ballgame from entertainment." If he shows, as he did in one episode, the burned corpse of a girl on a rock, it's "to drive home the point that this was a heinous crime and those responsible should be brought to the bar. We have access to many gruesome pictures we don't use."

• *Feature films.* There is a sense among survey respondents that feature films are getting away with murder. There is no question, insiders say, that features with higher budgets portray more vivid violence. Yet filmmakers and studio heads say the debate is having a big impact on the industry. "As always, studios and film executives are sensitive to what plays in the marketplace," says Tri-Star Pictures President Marc Platt. He cites his studio's Robert De Niro feature, *Mary Shelley's Frankenstein.* According to Platt, "That film, given the nature of the material and inherent creepiness, could run the gamut of very graphic gore. Even in 1991, the same movie might have been more graphic. We made sure that there is no part of the movie where you want to cover your eyes."

• *Cable TV.* Half the survey respondents feel cable portrays more violence than broadcast television, but network and cable officials have been cool toward each other since August 1993, when an industry "summit" on the issue was held. Differences exist even between basic and pay cable services. "Almost none of this applies to us, because we are a network that only gets into the home if the subscriber invites us there," explains Winston "Tony" Cox, chairman and CEO of Showtime Networks Inc. After the cable industry agreed to Illinois senator Paul Simon's demand for an independent violence monitor, broadcasters grudgingly were forced to follow suit. Each industry is seeking its own monitor. The cable industry supports the idea of putting technology into TVs allowing parents to control what their kids watch and using program ratings similar to those that exist for movies (such as "G" or "PG-13"), but broadcasters do not. Since each has its own trade group, no overall industry leader has emerged.

Roadblocks to Change

An even more fundamental problem than deciding who and what should be under scrutiny is determining what constitutes "gratuitous" violence. For example, in the *U.S. News*–UCLA survey, many respondents said that they might object to everything from shootings and stabbings to car accidents—depending on the circumstances. Without a clear definition of the problem, fixing it remains elusive.

Many Hollywood insiders say privately these discussions present the biggest roadblocks to real change. "Whenever the conversation gets a little hot and heavy, it's always, at bottom, a dispute about what constitutes violence and what kinds of programming ought we be concerned about," says one high-level executive who has participated in many industrywide meetings. In the meantime, even the networks may fall back on good old finger counting—a screenwriter pitching an original murder mystery to one network was turned down with the line, "We have to save our murders for the true stories."

"Network and cable companies have stepped up antiviolence messages."

Insiders say attempts at dialogue with Washington until recently have not gone smoothly. A fall 1993 dinner meeting at the Willard Hotel in Washington between network executives, advertising reps, actors and Attorney General Janet Reno—an event now famous due to actor Michael Moriarty's public denunciation of Reno—came about because the attorney general had indicated she might have spoken too soon when she testified against television before Congress. But Moriarty was not the only one at the session who felt the Justice contingent was hostile to Hollywood. "Reno even said she didn't watch much TV," says one. But the attorney general, who recalls a "spirited back-and-forth" exchange, points out she has continued to meet with network leaders. Other industry figures say their relationship and communication with Washington are improving. In March 1994, eight television executives met with President Clinton. The result, says Showtime's Cox, was a commitment to ongoing dialogue—and Clinton's MTV appearance. In addition, some congressional leaders, Warner's Moonves reports, have had kind words for the industry's recent activities.

What ultimately frustrates TV executives most is that they are seen as monsters when, in reality, they only provide what people want to buy. As Lily Tomlin says, it's "show *business*," not "show art." The respondents to the *U.S. News*–UCLA survey named viewers and ratings pressure as most responsible for encouraging violence on television.

> **"Without a clear definition of the problem, fixing it remains elusive."**

This may be even more true now because networks are owned by bottom-line-conscious corporations like Capital Cities and General Electric. Lee Rich, former chief of Lorimar, says NBC promised to support his family drama *Against the Grain* at the start of the 1993 season no matter what the ratings because it was a "quality" show. Those promises, says Rich, "were crap. The networks are into numbers, numbers, numbers." After eight episodes, *Against the Grain* failed to win top ratings in its time slot and was replaced by the action series *Viper*. Responds NBC's Ohlmeyer: "It was my favorite show. But I can't force people to come to the set."

Mixed Messages from the Public

So what does the public really want? ABC tried to determine that through a series of parent focus groups. "In the abstract, they all said they objected to too much violence," says Christine Hikawa, vice president of broadcast standards and practices. But none of the viewers objected to violent scenes, such as one from a TV movie of a woman being stalked and then accidentally murdered in a rape. Even ratings show a mix of interests: While the top movie for the 1993 season was the gentle Hallmark Hall of Fame *To Dance with the White Dog* on CBS, a TV movie of the real-life parricide by the Menendez brothers won Fox its highest rating ever for an original TV movie. Newsmagazine shows, too, see ratings soar with Charles Manson and Jeffrey Dahmer interviews.

On the feature film side, though, marketing and sales pressures these days most often favor nonlethal fare, and in recent years studios have produced ever-greater numbers of family-oriented films. A study by Los Angeles–based Exhibitor Relations shows the cumulative domestic box office total for the 52 PG-13 films released in 1993 at more than $1.7 billion; the 53 R-rated films earned $1.4 billion. Studios collected an additional $1.1 billion for 34 PG films. Some credit film company executives' growing families for the emphasis on family-friendlier fare, but more say it's a bid for a bigger audience. "We've cut the bloodshed not because of Congress but because we want a PG-13 rating," says Mace Neufeld, producer of the thriller *Clear and Present Danger*, with Harrison Ford. "We'll get a wider audience."

> *"What ultimately frustrates TV executives most is that they are seen as monsters when . . . they only provide what people want."*

This doesn't mean an end to action movies—or major action stars. Bruce Willis recently signed for the third installment of *Die Hard*, and Jean-Claude Van Damme plays the title role in the film version of the popular video game *Street Fighter*. In fact, actors who have tried to switch from guns to grins say audiences don't buy it. Sylvester Stallone bombed when trying comedy (*Oscar*; *Stop! Or My Mom Will Shoot*) but bounced back with *Cliffhanger* and *Demolition Man*. What makes a success, says Stallone, "is the perfect blending of men and material. But I don't think anyone's ever going to accept me in a comedy—ever, ever, ever. I'm a commodity. If you go to the store and grab a can of Stallone, you open it up and see Steve Martin—you don't want that."

A Moral Imperative

While Hollywood argues that the future of programming and films ultimately rests in the hands of audiences, President Clinton and others stress the industry's moral imperative to restrict violent content. What might be entertaining to individuals with ties to the community and family, says Clinton, may have an entirely different effect on others: For "people who have never been taught to understand the consequences of their action . . . these things can unintentionally set forth a chain reaction of ever more impulsive behavior." Under those criteria, responds filmmaker Stone: "You might never have films like *Schindler's List*, where heads were blown off, that take risks, that are important to show."

Ultimately, Congress may settle for industrywide self-policing. That would allow politicians to avoid the messy task of defining "gratuitous violence" and wrestling with First Amendment concerns. If anything, observes UCLA's Cole, the *U.S. News*–UCLA poll should reassure Congress and the public that the industry itself "is not satisfied with the status quo and the majority want a socially activist TV industry."

Insiders point out that self-policing has generated dramatic results in the past; they point, for instance, to the deliberate effort in the mid-1980s to deglamorize drug use on screen. The state of public ire being what it is, Hollywood faces an uphill battle: convincing outsiders bent on intervention that the problems are being seriously addressed. Until then, the message from Washington: We're looking at you, kid.

Prosocial Programming by the Media Can Be Effective

by Barbara Hattemer and Robert Showers

About the authors: *Barbara Hattemer is the president of the National Family Foundation, an organization that studies families and promotes ways to strengthen them. Robert Showers is an attorney. They are the authors of the book* Don't Touch That Dial, *from which this viewpoint is excerpted.*

> Mankind has always recognized the importance of entertainment and its values in rebuilding the bodies and souls of human beings.

> —The Motion Picture Code, 1930–1966

The American entertainment industry dominates the world market, controlling over 75 percent of the world's television, music, films, and radio programs. We are exporting more than democracy and free market economy to Eastern Europe, Russia, and Third World countries.

Democracy and Moral Degradation

Recent meetings with the World Council of Churches in Geneva, the Ecumenical Patriarch of the Orthodox Church in Constantinople, and the Pope in Rome raised a disturbing question. "Is it possible to have democracy *without* moral degradation, true freedom *without* sexual exploitation of women and children? Will the sex and violence shown in American media now be acted out on the streets of Eastern Europe and the Russian Republics?" European authorities came to a sobering conclusion, "If the price of freedom and democracy is our children's lives and our families' safety, the price is too high."

Americans face an even more poignant question at home: "Can democracy and freedom continue to exist *with* moral degradation and a destructive value system?" George Washington and French historian Alexis de Tocqueville did not think so. In his farewell address, Washington declared that a basic morality was essential to political prosperity. A generation later de Tocqueville said, "It is their mores, then, that make the Americans . . . capable of maintaining the rule of democracy."

On a very basic level, American media are promoting ideas, attitudes, and behaviors that either undergird or undermine democracy. There is a marked difference between license and responsible freedom, which would be better served by promoting the values on which this country was founded than by the current "anything goes" mentality. Said Ted Baehr,

> Film is not an enemy but a tool that can be used for good or evil. We must redeem the mass media so that through them we can communicate the good, the true and the beautiful to our children, American society and the world.

Clearly, television, films, magazines, and music have become powerful influences in our culture. They do much more than entertain. They can change time-honored cultural attitudes and replace them with destructive attitudes, or they can re-enforce positive attitudes, cultural values, and moral behaviors. Most researchers agree that entertainment media have unlimited potential for good that is virtually untapped. We will look at a variety of ways the media are helping to influence people in positive directions.

Finding Missing Children

According to Ernest Allen, president of the National Center for Missing and Exploited Children (NCMEC), "The media can be the best friend the parents of a missing child can have." The incredible power of the media can be harnessed in a matter of hours to capture the attention of the entire nation, find a missing child, expose a most-wanted criminal, or solve a mystery that has long stumped authorities. An emotionally presented television news piece can burn a child's smiling face into the consciences of the country and move people thousands of miles away to join the search for a child they will never know.

The media have helped to raise the level of awareness about the tragedy of child abduction and molestation to a height no advertising budget could match. Made-for-television movies about the disappearance of Etan Patz and the abduction and murder of Adam Walsh have touched the hearts of Americans nationwide. Each time *Adam* was rebroadcast, NBC presented a two-minute role-call of photographs of fifty missing children. A mere thirty seconds' television exposure per child yielded seven thousand calls that located twenty children. The growth in awareness from media exposure has helped the NCMEC recover 17,300 of 28,000 missing or sexually exploited children since 1984 and has resulted in over eighty successful prosecutions of child pornographers.

"Film is not an enemy but a tool that can be used for good or evil."

No medium can convey valuable information in a more attractive, entertaining way than television. The NCMEC and many other groups are now working directly with television networks to place valuable information in entertainment programs. An excellent example of prosocial programming that provided good family entertainment was *The Secret*, aired on CBS in April 1992. Touching the hearts of all who watched, this movie addressed adult illiteracy and sent special encouragement to those who had difficulty reading because of dyslexia. . . .

The Importance of Family

It is chic today to redefine the family. The media has helped by promoting all manner of living arrangements outside of marriage. It has portrayed family pathology so graphically, family appears to be the problem, not the solution to the nation's problems. But strong families have always been the strength of civilizations. It is when family bonds are weakened that society unravels and declines.

If even a handful of media executives could recognize how much the American family needs help and catch the vision of how prosocial programming could be developed to strengthen family values, there is no end to what they could do toward influencing for good the attitudes of the coming generation. Most producers, writers, and TV executives strongly believe that television entertainment should be a major force for social reform. With the increase in abnormal sex, blatant sexuality, and graphic violence during the past years, we must ask, reform in what direction, and what kind of society is their goal?

If money is the motive for the increase in sex and violence, even industry executives are recognizing it is time for a change. A 1991 *Forbes* magazine article by Norm Alster entitled "Crude Doesn't Sell" points out the enormous success basic cable

> *"No medium can convey valuable information in a more attractive, entertaining way than television."*

is having with old-fashioned family programs. Basic cable's audience share is up 33 percent while the networks' share dropped another 4 points in 1990, for a total of 25 percent since 1980. Alster reports surveys by Turner Broadcasting that show viewers eighteen to fifty-four "are absolutely opposed to [sexually] explicit television programming."

Family viewing hours, Saturday cartoons without ads and violence, and other approaches are being explored by Congress, the Federal Communications Commission, and media executives. Indications are that prosocial programming stressing pro-family values will be profitable for the industry as well as salutary for the culture.

A Window on the World

Dr. Dorothy G. Singer, co-director of Yale University Family Television Research Center, believes the media, particularly television, could provide role models for adolescents and teach them coping skills for everyday problems. Her research reveals that children are less concerned with drugs and sensational issues than they are with everyday concerns like how to maintain a close, intimate relationship with a friend and what to do about such things as lying and cheating in school, peer pressure, and grades. She said students are saying "we're really worried about our day to day existence: who is my friend . . . how do I come across to other people?"

In the past, the closeness of extended families provided the child with direct observation of their parents and other relatives in adult roles. Such opportunities are infrequent in today's more separated families. Television is now their "prime window on the world of adulthood," [Singer concludes].

> *"Most producers, writers, and TV executives strongly believe that television entertainment should be a major force for social reform."*

Researchers have found a direct relationship between stressful life events and delinquent behavior and substance abuse. Adolescent males in mother-only households are more likely to make decisions without direct parental input and are more likely to exhibit deviant behavior. Teen-agers' uncritical viewing of available programming puts them at risk of developing negative attitudes and imitating harmful behavior. Dr. Singer recommends the creation of more entertaining and thought-provoking shows designed to help teens think critically and develop problem-solving strategies.

The Degrassi Experiment

In order to test how thoughtful programming would affect young people's attitudes and behaviors, Dr. Singer showed five programs from the PBS [Public Broadcasting System] *Degrassi Junior High* series to fifth- to eighth-grade students. These programs were intended as an alternative to the situation comedies produced in Hollywood where precocious, "well-adjusted," witty young people are presented in designer clothing, living in beautiful surroundings, and parented by loving, understanding adults. The *Degrassi* series attempted to portray the complex experiences of early adolescence with insight, humor, compassion, and respect and to offer ideas and suggestions for long-term improvement rather than artificial quick solutions.

The programs have continuing characters but no "star." Different characters confront a particular dilemma each week. The audience has an opportunity to identify with youths like themselves or someone they would like to be. The situations selected included alcoholism in the family, parent-child relationships, lying, dating, dealing with handicaps, shyness, jealousy, shoplifting, judgment, decision-making, peer pressure, and sexual harassment.

Dr. Singer's subjects found they liked the PBS series and substantially increased their viewing of the *Degrassi* programs at home. One of the major discoveries of the experiment was the extremely positive effect of teacher-student discussions after viewing.

While four of the five episodes were well received, the one that made the children uncomfortable, confused, and disgusted was an experience of sexuality and adult-child intimacy, suggesting once again the negative effect on children of the large amount of sexual content in today's media.

The long success of *Little House on the Prairie* is an example of a program that put forth strong family values, provided good role models, and addressed issues relevant to today's world. A more recent program, *Beverly Hills 90210*, deals with problems pertinent to today's teen-agers and is receiving top ratings with this age group. There is good reason to believe such programs can be a financial success and have a positive influence on families at the same time.

Prosocial Programming

Showing children possible ways of coping with everyday problems should be one of the priorities of television in the future. There has been a great deal of research done on "prosocial programming." Broadly defined, this term has been applied to anything that benefits an individual or society at large.

Dr. J. Philippe Rushton reviewed thirty-five research studies of filmed prosocial behavior. He found that television influences behavior in the direction of the content of the program. An audience that sees friendliness and kindness modeled will accept it as appropriate, normative behavior. If, however, the audience frequently sees uncontrolled aggression and anti-social behaviors, it will come to accept this as the norm. He concluded, "Viewers learn from watching television and what they learn depends on what they watch."

A particular way of responding can be learned by watching others on film and identifying with them as they experience a situation. For example, children who experienced strong emotional arousal as they watched an episode of Lassie's master's risking his life to save Lassie's puppy, strongly responded when given an opportunity to help puppies in distress in a later experiment.

Dr. Rushton summarized fourteen separate studies that demonstrated the potential therapeutic value of television to reduce fear. Watching specially constructed films has reduced children's fears of dogs, snakes, hospital surgery, and social interaction. Such films have reduced the anxiety of high-school students in taking tests and the fear of dental treatment in adults.

Even children's self-control can be affected by what they watch on television. Studies of cheating on games, touching forbidden toys, and delaying gratification demonstrated that behavior could be influenced in either a positive or negative direction. Programs could be designed to help young people increase their resistance to temptation in a world that entices them with forbidden pleasures. There is substantial evidence that programs which strengthen children's internalized standards of right and wrong, rather than chipping away at them, could help restore our declining cultural standards.

> *"Prosocial programming stressing pro-family values will be profitable for the industry as well as salutary for the culture."*

Educational television has been a fruitful field for the study of the effects of prosocial programming. Children's Television Workshop programs "have demonstrated the potential of TV programming for children's social, intellectual and emotional development," [according to Dr. R.W. Winett].

Sesame Street, the most watched educational television program in history, regularly holds 75 percent of two- to five-year-olds in rapt attention. Solid research evidence reveals increased pre-reading skills and positive social skills and attitudes, made even stronger with parental discussion and encouragement.

Feeling Good, a primetime PBS program designed to motivate viewers to take responsibility for improving their health, was successful in changing simple but strategic health behaviors.

3-2-1 Contact achieved its first-year goals of helping children to enjoy science and to participate in scientific activities.

Freestyle successfully changed nine- to twelve-year-olds' perceptions of sex roles and career options in a less traditional direction. Girls became more independent and athletic, boys more nurturing.

Over Easy, which sought to reverse negative images of aging by using positive role models, produced an important guideline: use upbeat programming focusing on preventive behaviors rather than crisis intervention.

> *"Showing children possible ways of coping with everyday problems should be one of the priorities of television."*

Viewers of *As We See It* became more accepting of desegregation than nonviewers and more readily accepted members of other ethnic groups as friends or co-workers.

Modeling programs have successfully motivated consumers to conserve energy, refuse cigarettes, and resist advertising.

Mister Rogers' Neighborhood, which stresses children's social and emotional development, combines entertainment with education to emphasize themes like cooperation, sharing, sympathy, affection, friendship, understanding others' feelings, controlling aggression, and coping with frustration. A 1976 study found significant increases in social contacts and in giving positive attention to others for all children who watched the program. These and other studies have demonstrated that watching friendly behavior on television increases friendly behavior in real life.

The Effects of Prosocial Programming

In 1982 an important study found that prosocial programs could influence children with behavior disorders. These children normally chose to watch action and violent programs and acted out much of what they saw. During the experiment, they were shown programs containing at least twenty-nine prosocial acts and less than three aggressive acts per hour. The children who viewed the prosocial programs showed an increase in their concern for the interests of others while those children who watched the action and violent programs showed a decrease in this regard. *It also found that prosocial programming held children's attention as well as violent programs.*

Researchers like Dr. R.J. Harris have concluded that even when statistical proof of immediate behavioral change is lacking, prosocial programming lays the groundwork for later behavior change. It stimulates conversation with family, friends, or a doctor and opens the door for meaningful exchanges between parents and teens during dinner table conversation.

> *"Programs which strengthen children's internalized standards of right and wrong . . . could help restore our declining cultural standards."*

According to Dr. Harris, a commercial ad that affects 1 to 10 percent of consumers is considered extremely successful, and affecting even a small percentage of a mass audience is a substantial accomplishment. Dr. Harris suggests targeting those most receptive to attitude and behavior change in a positive direction, rather than those least likely to change. Therefore, prosocial programming designed to uphold and strengthen family values should be aimed at Americans who are unknowingly adopting the attitudes of a hedonistic society rather than at pornography addicts who deliberately seek hard-core material. Prosocial programming can be most effective for children and teen-agers who are trying to learn right from wrong and good from bad without the benefit of moral teaching and models from family, school, and church.

Prosocial television heightens awareness of a problem and helps the viewer perceive it differently. Once made aware of a problem by prosocial television, the viewer is more likely to pay attention the next time he hears a similar message and to be receptive to other influences in the same direction.

To successfully drive home the message, Dr. Winett suggests the use of multiple models, similar to the target audience but a bit more competent, portrayed in a range of situations that show the model being reinforced for the appropriate social behavior. Dramatic stories that show variations of the desired behavior and an accurate portrayal of the obstacles that can be expected help viewer identification. Discussion helps to insure that the message is not lost.

The most dramatic scenes are the easiest to recall. Therefore, these are the best in which to imbed the intended message. [Jerome Johnston and James S. Ettema conclude that] "the drama must be so intimately related to the intended lesson that they cannot be understood apart from each other. More than that, the drama must be the lesson."

Saying "No" to Sex

Researchers [Bryant, Alexander, and Brown] have concluded that "viewers can and do learn from educational television. . . . The evidence of success with children as the target audience appears to be overwhelming." Similar achievements with teen-agers and adults are possible if educators, researchers, and television producers poll what they have learned. Working together, they can make effective stories that model desirable behavior for specific audiences.

For example, saying no can be modeled effectively. What a fourteen-year-old girl will do when pressured by a boy in the back seat of a car or what the young man will do if she is reluctant might depend on the television images that flash through their minds at that moment. Will there be twelve thousand images of sex outside of marriage from the past three years of television and movie viewing or will there be models of delayed gratification and unselfish caring?

In recommending prosocial programming to the television and film industry, we narrowly define it as programming that espouses family values—those values that strengthen the concept of marriage and child rearing as primary in maintaining a healthy society.

Prosocial programming so defined can be very entertaining. It can include great drama, deliriously funny comedy, and spine-tingling mystery. It requires the development of a value scheme, a systematic set of parameters, and limitations that guide the writer and director in drawing the line. Without limiting the entertainment value of the work, social value is added. Rather than limiting appeal, it increases the appeal for much of the audience.

An overall social policy promoting marriage and healthy family life in institutions throughout the country is needed to bolster the faltering American family. No institution is better able to communicate that policy to children, adolescents, and adults than the enterprising and innovative American communications media; and no medium could do it better than television. Dr. Winett foreshadowed the conclusions of the National Family Foundation Media Workshop when he declared, "Television that models socially valued behaviors, responses, attitudes or beliefs . . . is television used to best advantage."

Ratings Systems Can Curb Violence in Video Games

by Gregg Keizer

About the author: *Gregg Keizer is a contributing editor to* Omni *magazine, a monthly periodical that focuses on science and futuristic topics.*

They're the best evidence yet that the apocalypse is upon us. They promote violence among kids; they play to our most prurient interests; they have less socially redeeming value than a 24-hour stretch of MTV.

No, we're not talking about Beavis and Butt-head. We're talking about videogames, the things that put Sonic and Mario on school lunchboxes.

Digital fun and its impact made the news, big time, late in 1993. Whether it was in the cold and often uninformed questioning of a Senate hearing or in the after-Christmas-sale-style rush of publishers to defend their products, the face of censorship peeked through the pixels of electronic entertainment.

When the going got tough before the Senate Judiciary and Government Affairs Committee, game publishers got ratings religion. Faced with the prospect of government controls, a coalition of publishers and dealers proposed a regime of self-censorship, a ratings strategy that for all intents and purposes mirrored what Sega had established earlier. Games would be rated GA for a general audience, MA-13 for a more mature audience over 13, and MA-17 for those over 17. Even that wasn't enough to mollify Senator Joseph Lieberman (D, Connecticut), one of the committee's co-chairs, who called it "the least the videogame industry can do, not the best it can do."

The furor stems from the fact that—right or wrong—electronic entertainment is perceived as a kid thing. Ratings aren't enough, so the line goes, to keep violence- and sex-heavy games from poking phosphors through kids' eyes. Lieberman was adamant about that. "It would be far better for parents and kids if the industry simply kept the gory violence and sex out of their games," he said.

The senator's missing the point. Computer games and videogames are *not* just for kids any more than movies are just for preteens. Nor is a tiered ratings structure that caters to children's concerns a long-term solution, since—unlike relatively stable forms of entertainment such as films and music—digital games are a moving target. The market may be powered by videogames for kids now, but it won't be for long. Thanks to games on CD—for computers, for the more expensive machines like 3DO and SegaCD—and, when it comes along, to digital entertainment delivered over cable or phone lines, adults will soon be driving sales.

One Label for All

This is not to say there aren't games unfit for kids. There are. But there is a better way to handle the problem than a lock-step ratings system that, at best, is inconsistent and misleading. How else are we to describe a system that gives a shoot-'em-up like *Soldiers of Fortune* a GA but hands an MA-13 to a straightforward boxing game like Sega's *Prizefighter*?

Instead, publishers and retailers and parents' groups should get together and nail down one label: NC—"not for children." Games carrying adult themes and adult stories should be so marked. Retailers should enforce the rating, as theaters do now, by refusing to sell such games to anyone under 18.

As for other games, publishers should note content of their wares with clear phrases like "graphic violence" and "adult language" and be smart enough to advertise such games honestly. That means running ads in forums other than those aimed at kids—as are many videogame magazines and cable channels like Nickelodeon. It means being up-front in presentation, packaging, and box copy, not hiding a killing fest inside cartoon graphics, expecting the violence to be somehow less objectionable. That means providing some *real* information to anyone trying to determine what is or is not objectionable material for themselves or their children.

> *"Games carrying adult themes and adult stories should be so marked."*

It may not be a perfect system, but it does spread out the responsibility and make everyone, from publishers to parents, pay attention. It's not the easiest way out—that would be to just let someone *else* decide what's good and what's not—but it's the best way to ensure no one gets cut out of the electronic entertainment of today. And of the future.

Media Executives Do Nothing to Curb Violence

by Reed Irvine and Joseph C. Goulden

About the authors: *Reed Irvine is the head and founder of Accuracy in Media (AIM), a conservative organization that works to inform the public on media inaccuracies and bias. Joseph C. Goulden is the director of media analysis for AIM.*

Even the print media snickered in the summer of 1993 when the television industry and Hollywood essentially told Congress to "get lost" in the debate over the increased volume of televised gore which is splattering America's living rooms. A front-page analysis in the *New York Times* carried the headline "Mild Slap at TV Violence," and reporter Edmund L. Andrews correctly wrote that the networks "threw the smallest bone possible to their Congressional critics."

The "bone" is an innocuous warning label which the networks will put on shows which executives decide are overly violent. A *Washington Post* editorial suggested that the "labels may offer cover for more sensationalism and grisliness.". . .

A Direct Link

Film industry lobbyist Jack Valenti drew warm applause for his windy eloquence before a House subcommittee in denying that the violence slops out of TV and motion picture screens into real-live street crime. "Stretching from the early birth years of this Republic," Valenti declared, "violence has run through our history like a twanging scarlet wire . . ."

Oh, nonsense, retorted Dr. Leonard Eron, of the University of Michigan, who has studied TV violence since the 1950s. He told the same committee that on the link between TV and violence, "the scientific debate is over," that is, the connection is clear. Eron said that repeated studies have shown "a direct causal link between exposure to televised violence and subsequent aggressive behavior of the viewers."

The bottom line is that there is no reason to trust the TV industry to do any effective self-policing on televised violence. A researcher for Accuracy in Me-

Reed Irvine and Joseph C. Goulden, "Networks Can't Be Trusted," *Washington Inquirer*, July 9, 1993. Reprinted by permission.

dia (AIM) spent a week at the Library of Congress looking at how long Congress has fumbled around with the issue without anything really being done. We were surprised to learn that Congress held its first hearings on TV violence in June 1952—more than four decades ago. The concern then was the link between TV violence and the surge in juvenile crime in the years following World War Two.

The networks' answer for four decades was pretty much what it was when the entertainment moguls went before Congress in 1993—that movies, those shown on TV and in the theaters, cannot be assigned

> *"Hollywood has long been renowned for the zest with which it opens its pocketbooks for leftist Democrats."*

blame for all the violence in our society. The networks did promise to try to limit the amount of violence to which they subject kids. But they didn't want Congress or anyone else telling them what they could or could not show, because their shows enjoy the same First Amendment rights as the rest of the media.

Well, perhaps so, and we agree that government regulation isn't the solution to every problem that society faces. But the violence-on-television problem has persisted since the original 1952 hearings and, in fact, has intensified in recent years since the networks began competing with cable channels. Our AIM researcher counted no less than 27 hearings that Congress has conducted on TV violence. And each time Congress has looked at the issue, the television industry either denied any link between the violence on its screens and violence on the streets, or, conversely, promised to curb it.

Possible Solutions

So how much trust can we put in the new industry promises?

Dr. Eron said that the TV industry has "demonstrated over the last 20 years that it cannot or will not regulate itself." He urged that "something must be done before we expose a new generation of our youth" to the harm of televised violence.

Technology could help. A simple electronic chip known as a "V block" would enable parents to program TV sets to block out shows coded as violent. Television industry officials told Congress they don't like the idea. Warren Littlefield, head of NBC entertainment, said his network needed to show violence in dealing with "socially relevant issues, like incest, date rape, the danger of maniacal cult leaders." He expressed the fear that the V block would shut off programs with socially important messages on the grounds that they contain violence.

One solution already in effect in many Western European nations restricts TV violence during children's viewing hours—from six in the morning until ten at night. Unless the television industry does something on its own, it will face distasteful governmental regulation. Call us cynical, but we don't think the TV moguls have the sense to do the right thing.

Movie Ratings Are Ineffective

by *The Lancet*

About the author: The Lancet *is a weeky international journal of medical science and practice.*

After forty years of research and an international bibliography of over 3,000 studies, reviews, commentaries, and meta-analyses, it is clear that television violence can lead to harmful aggressive behaviour. "The scientific debate is over", Leonard D. Eron, a prominent research psychologist, told the US Congress in 1993. On April 2, 1992, residents of Washington, DC, who were watching television between 6 a.m. and midnight might have witnessed 138 murders, 333 gunfights, and nearly 175 stabbings and club attacks, according to researchers who switched on ten channels and began counting—and, in this area famous for crime, the statistics did not even include newscasts. From 6 a.m. to 9 a.m. there were 475 scenes of fictional violence (160/h), and an additional 574 violent acts (190/h) were broadcast between 2 p.m. and 5 p.m. These are television's "children's hours". Throughout the bloodshed, a veneer of physical and ethical sterility was preserved: half of all violence resulted in no injuries and the predictable wounds of another 25% of victims were left unseen; 83% of the violence was presented without judgment. According to investigators, no special programmes such as "slasher" films or "action-adventure" features were broadcast on that day: "The only thing that stands out about this day's schedule is its blandness", they observed. It is not surprising then that, after watching television for 2–4 h each day, American children will have witnessed 8,000 television murders and another 100,000 acts of violence by the time they have completed elementary school at age 11. In other countries there is similar cause for concern—not least because of the free exchange of films, television programmes, and video material directly or via satellite. Screen violence can be regarded as an international threat to the public health.

Despite decades of promises, the US television industry has shown little self-restraint. When Congress first investigated the issue in the 1950s, 16% of "prime time" programmes featured violence and crime. By 1961 the figure had increased to 50%. And in 1964, after finding still no improvement, Congressional investigators concluded that broadcasters were violating their own Code of Good Practice "with impunity".

> *"The US television industry has shown little self-restraint."*

From 1967 to 1990, though reports showing ill-effects of TV violence proliferated by the hundreds, the industry responded only by turning up the violence, and 70–80% of prime-time shows had at least one "overt actor threat to hurt or kill a person" [according to G. Gerbner and N. Signorelli]. The only significant change in the pattern of programming occurred during the 1980s era of deregulation, when the hourly rate of violence in network weekend children's shows increased by 36%. Industry leaders maintain that "only a small fraction of the programming on the four networks involves any violent content" [according to J. Federman]. And critics argue that violence counts are too subjective for science, that one viewer's violence is another viewer's drama. "Nature never draws a line that isn't smudged", Jack Valenti, an industry lobbyist, told Congress in October 1991. But the consistency of the data, and the informed opinions of bodies including the American Academy of Pediatrics, the American Psychological Association, and the American Psychiatric Association, point to the need for reform.

Weaknesses in Ratings System

In June 1993, under pressure from Congress, the networks undertook to broadcast "parental advisories" (i.e., warnings to parents) before transmission of programmes that, in their opinion, feature violence unsuitable for children. It would be too harsh to dismiss these promises as "too little, too late"; but we must also realise that the medium and its audience are changing. There is less network broadcasting in 1994 than meets the eye. Over half of American homes now receive cablecasts and 40% have video-cassette recorders. As these numbers grow, television screens will increasingly display the severe brand of violence once reserved for the local cinema; and a more informative ratings system is needed to accommodate the new onslaught. Unfortunately, the current system is a weak precedent. The rating of films in America is a strangely unencumbered process. The only qualification for selection to the Ratings Board of the Motion Picture Association of America is "parenthood". Its twelve anonymous members are paid from fees charged to movie producers and distributors who employ the Board to rate their work. Ratings are made on the basis of what is seen on screen "and not what is imagined or thought", and advisories and restrictions are delimited by ages 13 and 17. The task of the Board is to estimate how other American parents would rate the suitability of the same film for their children. "The entire rostrum of the rating program rests on the assumption of responsibility by parents. If parents don't care, or if they are languid in guiding their children's movie going, the rating system becomes useless," [states Jack Valenti].

The System Is Ineffective

The political and moral isolation of the American ratings process is dismaying. In a survey of ratings boards in 36 nations and provinces, the United States was the only country where parenthood was the sole qualification for membership. It is also the only nation where board members remain anonymous. Most other countries employ civil servants whose deliberations are public. Although the industry's "rostrum" may have been sturdy generations ago, today millions of American "latch-key" children return from school each day to poorly supervised or empty homes. Surely there can be more corporate effort—if not frank responsibility—to limit the violence these children are exposed to when they turn on their televisions in the late afternoon for human company. The current ratings process ignores decades of research in childhood development. For example, children's intellectual and emotional growth are not delimited by age 0–13 years, 13–17 years, and over 17 years. Important cognitive development occurs within the preteen years and may have a bearing on what a child absorbs and learns (and imitates) from a given act of violence. Moreover, the negative effects of programme content do not necessarily diminish with maturity. Preschoolers may be affected by monsters that adolescents laugh at, and adolescents may suffer from implied or off-screen violence that preschoolers ignore (two situations the US board does not consider). Finally, the context of violence seems to be as important as the quantity. Rewards, punishments, justifications, and consequences of violent activity are critical to children's understanding of it. Unfortunately, these psychological subtleties are unaddressed by the current US film ratings system, and there is no indication that television networks have a better plan.

Congress is considering measures to curb television violence. Among these is a proposal to restrict violent programming to evening "adult hours"—a limitation already in effect in the United Kingdom, Australia, Canada, and France. But First Amendment protections of free speech mean that such legislation will be difficult to pass. Indeed, any attempts at government control over the creative contour of the American airwaves will surely be headed for First Amendment conflict. Still, there are measures to be taken. Public health demands public education. Children can be taught "media literacy" so that they understand both the fictions and the effects of broadcast violence. And parents and teachers can be taught to select programmes appropriate for the ages of their children and to look for the untoward effects of exposure to television violence. New technologies that would allow parents to shield their homes from violent shows should also be considered. Finally, the ratings system must be made wholly independent of those who profit by its neglect.

The Film Industry Does Nothing to Curb Media Violence

by John Pilger

About the author: *John Pilger is the author of* Distant Voices *and other books. He is a columnist for* New Statesman & Society, *a British magazine of political and social opinion.*

Good Friday being cold and wet, I went to the movies. I bought *Time Out*, which advised that a "superb modern thriller" had arrived. This was *One False Move*, directed by Carl Franklin. "They hardly make 'em like this any more," wrote reviewer Geoff Andrew. "Don't miss it." What struck me was his reassurance that this was "mostly . . . an unexpectedly non-violent film".

The film I saw was a mindless, nauseating piece of work that made me want to take a bath. It was crudely directed and packed with so many inanities and stereotypes that their parade became almost a source of fascination. Above all, it produced such horrific and gratuitous violence that two women sitting next to me left, while a few seats along a group of young men giggled and whooped their way through every moment of orgiastic bloodletting. "While there are sudden spasms of action," waffled Geoff Andrew, "Franklin concentrates instead on moral relativism . . ."

Cinema and Its Criticism

Just as this film is typical of a new wave of violent junk now pouring out of Hollywood, so *Time Out* is not alone in its pretentious endeavour to elevate it. In the *Observer*, Philip French wrote that the director "performs with the skill of a master angler. He tightens and relaxes his line, but doesn't let us off the hook until we're pulled ashore at the end, gasping with some form of catharsis. There are strong echoes of *High Noon* . . ."

When a serious critic like Philip French makes such an idle, specious compar-

John Pilger, "Action, Camera, Bloodbath," *New Statesman & Society*, April 16, 1993.

ison, there is clearly something very wrong with the popular cinema and its criticism. *High Noon* was both a great moral fable and a true thriller that, in exploring the grand themes of courage and fear, relied upon a supreme sense of psychological menace. Like Hitchcock's films—*Psycho* included—it had minimal actual violence, because little was required.

In contrast, *One False Move* opens with two psychopaths slaughtering people at a party. We see Pluto, who is said to have the IQ of a genius, methodically covering the heads of his writhing victims with pillow cases, then stabbing them to death. The violence is casual, *normal*. While he does his work, a video camera is left on. "Sick bas-

> *"Hollywood's sludge of ultra-violence is now consuming film-making to the* **exclusion** *of all other ways of life."*

tard," comments a cop later. Yes; and the voyeurism allows us, the audience, to be "sick bastards", too.

The *Guardian* critic, Derek Malcolm, acknowledged that his own stomach almost turned at this scene, yet he went on to congratulate the film for being "in the business of making you think rather than sick", and to describe it as "brilliantly observed and subtly characterised". The two psychopaths go on to murder another five people. The one with a permanent scowl pours lighter fluid over a young woman, grabs her in the crotch and threatens to set her ablaze. Instead, he suffocates them all in plastic bags. Brilliantly observed; subtly characterised.

Meanwhile, down in Arkansas, Sheriff "Hurricane" Dixon manages to embody every known stereotype of the southern hick. He is a good guy, though, a Huck Finn who calls blacks niggers and doesn't mean it. And he has an apple-pie home. According to Philip French, this cartoon character has "a Faulknerian complexity". Meanwhile, Hurricane is being made fun of by two big city cops from LA—the usual buddies team: one black, one white. Little do we suspect that Hurricane is the daddy of the little boy of one of the psychopaths' girlfriends. She is black and the little boy is brown, which apparently helps to make this film "one-third social document" (Derek Malcolm).

Meanwhile, the killers do some more meaningful killing, with Pluto demonstrating how you slit a throat while running. As we approach the finale, "gasping with some form of catharsis" (P French), sullen black folks sit on stumps and porches, playing the blues on a harmonica and eating fried chicken. Of course, it ends in yet another bloodbath, with Hurricane no longer disowning his little brown son. Brilliantly observed; subtly characterised.

Designer Violence

The overwhelming majority of movies shown in this country [the United Kingdom] are American; and many are off the same assembly line as *One False Move*. That is to say, they are corrupt; they celebrate violence for the sake of it, and for a buck. They also promote the sexualisation of true violence, the kind that rapes and kills. In *One False Move*, one of the psychopaths holds a knife to his girlfriend's throat and she coos at him.

This is *chic*, designer violence that, wrote one critic, is "nothing worse than you read in the papers". It reflects reality, you see, just as, presumably, the *Dressed to Kill* series and, more recently, *Reservoir Dogs*, reflect life as we live it. The truth is that Hollywood's sludge of ultra-violence is now consuming film-making to the *exclusion* of all other ways of life. There is seldom a mirror held up to the violence of poverty that is endemic in the United States. That would be "too political". I remember Philip French dismissing the quirky, brave documentary film, *Roger and Me*, which, although flawed, shone a rare light on the violence of unemployment and eviction in America's industrial heartland. I recall that most critics overpraised *My Private Idaho*, in which the homeless were glamorised as a Falstaffian cabaret troupe.

I don't know if people become violent as a result of what they see on the screen. Perhaps no one knows. Yet when Stanley Kubrick saw the prima facie social effects of *A Clockwork Orange* he worried enough to withdraw it from distribution in this country. When David Puttnam saw *Midnight Express* on show in Times Square, New York, he had misgivings about "certain se-quences". And both those films were made in relatively innocent days. Now we have little choice. It is even difficult to find a PG-rated movie that is not violent, as I discovered re-cently when I took my eight-year-old daughter to see *Mr Nanny* and *Home Alone 2*. Both demonstrate the skill of directors in cynically "containing" the violence, while ensuring that the young in the audience are drenched in it.

> *"There is seldom a mirror held up to the violence of poverty that is endemic in the United States."*

The Meaning of Responsibility

Objecting to this should not be the preserve of the fundamentalist "family val-ues" right. Responsibility has a dictionary as well as an ideological meaning; and it applies to directors, actors and critics alike. We are awaiting the next round of riots in Los Angeles, where many of these films come from. How can a society that has the highest rate of gun-related crimes in the world, the highest rate of imprisonment in the world, not to mention the greatest social divisions, begin to cleanse itself of violence when the popular culture is consumed by it? What is the difference between cops beating up Rodney King in a snatched video and a movie like *One False Move* filmed in the same city?

What struck me when I first went to report the American war in Indochina was the way US marines—especially poor blacks and whites—acted out Holly-wood. In the wake of the My Lai massacre in 1969, I conducted a series of in-terviews with US soldiers who had murdered civilians. All but one of them re-ferred to war and crime movies as their cultural guide. Since then, Hollywood has raised and raised the ante.

How many directors give a damn about this, or have themselves been the victims of the very violence whose nihilism they aim pointblank at young males and which they hope will make them rich? A not dissimilar question might be put to the critics. It is they who normalise the unspeakable, who are part of the big sell; and the more pretentious their praise, the better. *One False Move*, wrote Philip French, has "undertones of Greek tragedy". The same film, wrote Geoff Andrew, has "the taut inexorability of Greek tragedy". There are a few honourable exceptions, such as Barry Norman, who have consistently refused to accept violence for the sake of it. But when the pack is generally united, who spots the charlatan? Who dares to say the emperor—that is, much of the film industry—has no clothes?

Chapter 4

What Should Be Done About Media Violence?

CURRENT CONTROVERSIES

Addressing Media Violence: An Overview

by Elizabeth Jensen and Ellen Graham

About the authors: *Elizabeth Jensen and Ellen Graham are staff reporters for the* Wall Street Journal.

When Attorney General Janet Reno took television broadcasters to task in October 1993 for violent programming, it was but the latest round in 40 years of government sword-rattling over the medium's power over children. Despite decades of anguish, however, neither the government nor programmers have figured out what to do about televised violence.

Violence on television, and risky copycat behavior is as old as the medium itself. The original 1950s *Superman* series incited a few children to leap off rooftops in imitation of the soaring star, helping set the stage for the first congressional TV-violence hearings. Today, much of the violence on television has moved away from network series onto news and newsmagazine shows and, especially, onto cable, where movies and music videos often glorify and eroticize brutality.

TV violence has traditionally been measured quantitatively, by researchers who count incidents of real or threatened physical injury. This essentially gives equal weight to Bugs Bunny bopping Elmer Fudd with a carrot and an Uzi-armed psychopath picking off a terrorized and helpless victim.

The Type of Violence Is Important

Most such analyses show a fairly stable level of prime-time violence over the past 25 years—or five incidents per hour, says University of Delaware researcher Nancy Signorelli, though she adds that the most recent study found mayhem in fewer shows. Many critics, however, believe there is a more dangerous qualitative change toward violence that seems more realistic and more glamorous.

"We need to get beyond simple counts of physical injury and look at the context," says Edward Donnerstein, professor of communications at the University of California at Santa Barbara. He draws a distinction between violence in acclaimed miniseries like *Roots* or *Holocaust*, and gratuitous brutality shown in movies like *The Terminator* or *Friday the 13th*, which are shown unedited on pay-cable channels. The latter kind of violence is what is so troubling to policy makers and viewers, he says, lamenting that content analysis of television still doesn't measure the type of violence being shown.

> *"The original 1950s* **Superman** *series incited a few children to leap off rooftops in imitation of the soaring star."*

Michael Dann, a veteran network programmer who started at NBC in 1950 and ran CBS Entertainment in the late 1960s, has testified nine times before Congress on television violence, defending everything from Westerns to police shows. He argues that series television is less violent today than at any time since the 1950s. What has changed, he suggests, is reality. Not only is society itself more violent today, but "local news, network news, the front page of the newspaper and magazines" reflect that violence back into the nation's living rooms. "I have never seen so much real-world coverage of violence, separate from entertainment programming, as now," he says.

The endlessly replayed video footage of the Rodney King and Reginald Denny beatings in Los Angeles are obvious examples of brutal reality footage. Dr. Donnerstein observes that, unlike gratuitous fictionalized violence—calculated to elicit cheers from audiences—such news programming depresses most viewers. "We see the real injury, and people are bothered," he says, "and that's a much, much different situation."

Together, ABC, CBS, NBC and Fox devote nine prime-time hours a week to news magazines [in 1993], up from just two hours in the early 1980s. Crime is a frequent topic on such shows. Fox, a unit of News Corp., also has a slate of "reality" shows, including *America's Most Wanted* and *Cops*, which also are credited with occasionally apprehending criminals. Local stations' news programs are filled with crime stories, as are promotional spots teasing late-night newscasts. All add to the perception that prime-time is violent.

When it comes to entertainment shows, ABC, CBS and NBC have only a handful of series that contain sporadic violence. Among them are *NYPD Blue* from ABC, a unit of Capital Cities/ABC Inc., and *Walker, Texas Ranger* from CBS Inc.'s CBS network. One reason: In recent years, situation comedies have delivered better Nielsen ratings than action-adventure shows.

A list of children's top-10 prime-time shows in 1982–83 contained four adventure programs, including NBC's exceedingly violent *A-Team*. Today, by contrast, the kids' top-10 list includes only sitcoms.

Amy Fisher and David Koresh

Currently, the most violent content found on the networks is in lurid made-for-television movies, chronicling everything from the saga of Amy Fisher [a high school student who shot her lover's wife] to the government's siege at [Branch Dividian] cult leader David Koresh's Waco, Texas, headquarters. But even these are not as violent as many of the uncut movies shown on cable, where standards-and-practices executives (the industry's in-house censors) tend to give producers more creative freedom. It is also mostly on cable that reruns of old Westerns and police dramas have found new life. Cable network Comedy Central is even parodying the uproar over violent television: It plans to launch "Drive-In Reviews," rating the most-violent moments on film.

Network executives at the October 1993 hearing on the issue were frustrated by the number of questioners who prefaced their remarks with, "I don't watch much television, but . . ."

"All we're asking for is to be scrutinized for what we put on the air," says Rosalyn Weinman, vice president of broadcast standards and practices at General Electric Co.'s NBC. She adds that the network is fully prepared to defend its programs. But she adds: "We're being tarred with the brush of the entire media landscape, of which we're a small part, and the part with most checks and balances."

Blame *Bonnie and Clyde*

David Bianculli, television critic for the *New York Daily News*, thinks Ms. Weinman has a point. Washington isn't making a sufficiently clear distinction between programming on the networks, syndication and cable, he says. Taking broadside potshots at televised violence, he says, "is a no-lose situation for politicians. There's no lobby saying violence is good." (Recent polls show that more than 80% of the public is concerned about media violence.)

Network-TV violence peaked in the 1980s with *Miami Vice*, reruns of which are aired in syndication, Mr. Bianculli says. He and other media watchers blame cable and its unedited Hollywood movies for the violence problem. The original early-1960s network series *The Untouchables* was about as raw as either TV or movies got up to that time, Mr. Bianculli says. But a few years later the film *Bonnie and Clyde* was released, and Hollywood took a quantum leap beyond TV in violent content—a lead he says movies have held ever since.

> *"The most violent content found on the networks is in lurid made-for-television movies."*

The University of California's Dr. Donnerstein believes the issue of TV violence has assumed its current urgency because of the medium's intrusiveness in the home. "The big change in the past decade is children's access to cable, video on demand, rental videos and other media through the TV box," he says.

A number of legislators appear determined to find ways to regulate TV violence, particularly on the broadcast networks, despite obvious First Amendment hurdles. Among the proposals: Providing a "safe harbor" [time period] that excludes violent shows while kids are likely to be watching; ordering the Federal Communications Commission to force broadcast station licensees and cable franchisees to label shows containing violence or unsafe gun practices; and instructing the FCC to issue quarterly report cards on the levels of violence on TV.

Attorney General Reno raised eyebrows when she testified in October 1993 that the proposed bills would be constitutional. Robert S. Peck, legislative counsel for the American Civil Liberties Union, argues that none of the bills would pass constitutional muster; he cites a long list of cases to back up his point.

Amid the clamor, the *Daily News*'s Mr. Bianculli offers some historical perspective: Back in the 1920s, it seems that a furor arose over a child who had killed his father with a carving knife after watching a silent movie. Of the incident, G.K. Chesterton wrote at the time: "This may possibly have occurred, though if it did, anybody of common sense would prefer to have details of that particular child, rather than about that particular picture."

Increased Government Regulation of Media Violence Is Necessary

by William S. Abbott

About the author: *William S. Abbott is an attorney and the president of the National Foundation to Improve Television, a public interest, nonprofit educational organization dedicated to reducing television violence.*

Despite more than two decades of policy statements and announcements of programming guidelines by the broadcast networks and the cable television industry, television programming in the United States remains undeniably violent. The television industry's recent promises to set up a violence-monitoring system, and for cable programming a violence ratings system, sound good, but the evidence on the continuing high level of prime-time television violence suggests that stronger measures are needed. Also, the television industry's track record suggests that these promises are unlikely to be kept without governmental oversight and increased public attention to the problem.

Findings over the last 20 years by three different Surgeons General, the Attorney General's Task Force on Family Violence, the American Medical Association, the National Institute of Mental Health, the American Psychiatric Association, the American Psychological Association, the American Academy of Pediatrics, and other medical authorities indicate that televised violence is harmful to all of us, but particularly to the mental health of children.

Severe Behavioral Impact

In 1987 the Medical Director of the American Psychiatric Association, expressing the association's support of Congressional efforts to reduce the level of violence on television, stated: "The evidence is overwhelming that violence in television programming can have a negative and severe behavioral impact on young people and adults. As medical professionals, we feel an obligation to counsel against adverse health effects when sufficient scientific evidence supports such a viewpoint." In 1990, the American Academy of Pediatrics issued a policy statement encouraging all pediatricians to advise parents to limit their children's television viewing to one or two hours per day at most due to the scientific consensus surrounding the hazards of viewing television violence.

US citizens of all ages and backgrounds watch astoundingly large amounts of television. In our urban centers an average family views 77 hours per week. In these families' homes, a television set is on an average of 11 hours per day. One indication of how strongly television influences children's lives is the estimate that by the time many American children graduate from high school they will have watched television for approximately 22,000 hours, twice as many hours as they will have spent in school.

It is clear that millions of our children today are looking more to television than the schools for role models and value systems that they will come to adopt. It is also clear that many of these children are watching violent programming without any supervision or guidance. A study completed in 1991 for the Corporation for Public Broadcasting found that 47 percent of surveyed children, aged six to seventeen, had a television set in their own room. Only 50 percent of these children reported that their parents set any rules at all regarding their television viewing.

"Television programming in the United States remains undeniably violent."

Despite the television industry's assurances, there is no indication that television has recently altered its emphasis on violent fare. A special study commissioned by *TV Guide* in April 1992 was designed to assess the content of contemporary television programming. The Center for Media and Public Affairs, a nonprofit monitoring company, was enlisted to tape, tabulate, computerize, and analyze the programming of ten Washington, DC, channels for an 18-hour period (6 a.m. to midnight) on April 2, 1992. The ten channels were the local affiliates of ABC, CBS, NBC, Fox and PBS; one non-affiliated station, WDCA; plus the cable channels of WTBS, the USA Network, MTV and HBO.

TV Guide noted that the program schedules during the 18-hour period "were notable only for their ordinariness: no untypically violent movies like *Rambo* or *Scarface* were shown; even the news was light on violent events. . . ." The conclusion that *TV Guide* draws from the evidence obtained in this study is inescapable: "violence remains a pervasive, major feature of contemporary television programming and it's coming from more sources and in greater volume than ever before."

More Evidence of Increased Violence

The National Coalition on Television Violence conducted studies in the mid-1980s of 18 networks on broadcast and cable television and found, "[T]he advent of cable TV, instead of decreasing the average consumption of violent entertainment, has increased the intake of violence by an average of 50 percent for families subscribing to a pay cable movie channel."

During February and March of 1994, prime-time programming from the major broadcasters included extremely violent movies such as *Lethal Weapon 2, Out for Justice, Hard to Kill, Sudden Impact,* and *Marked for Death.* For the week of March 7–12, 1994, USA Network won the distinction of being the most-watched cable network in the country for the week, in large part by featuring the *First Blood, Rambo, First Blood Part 2,* and *Rambo III* trilogy as prime-time and Sunday afternoon fare.

The evidence that there is a causal relationship between television violence and violence in real life is overwhelming. Three different methods have been used to study the relationship between television viewing and aggressive behavior. Evidence from laboratory experiments has overwhelmingly indicated that children who watch a film with aggressive content imitate aggressive behavior seen in the film, show an increase in other forms of aggressive behavior, and are subsequently more aggressive than children who see either a "neutral" film or no film at all.

Field Studies and Longitudinal Studies

Field studies on children in various countries and settings have also shown a link between aggressive behavior and exposure to television violence. Aletha Hudson, co-director and co-founder of the Center for Research on the Influence of Television on Children, reported in her study for the Surgeon General's Advisory Committee on Television and Social Behavior, that over a nine-week period, groups of four-year-old children who were shown cartoons containing violence (*Batman* and *Superman*) "were subsequently more likely to hit other children, call people names, fail to obey classroom rules, and become impatient when they encountered minor frustrations" than two other groups of children shown either non-violent programs or "pro-social" programs emphasizing non-violent ways to resolve conflicts.

Researchers have also conducted so-called longitudinal studies, which track the relationship between viewing television violence and aggression over time. In a 22-year study of 875 children in a semi-rural New York county, University

"Televised violence is harmful to all of us."

of Michigan researchers L. Rowell Huesmann and Leonard D. Eron considered whether the television viewing habits of eight-year-old boys were related to later aggressive behavior and criminal acts which they committed by age 30. The results indicated that, even after controlling for the boys' aggressiveness, intelligence, and socio-economic status, at age eight, the boys' television violence viewing correlated significantly with the seriousness of the crime for which they were convicted by age 30. The study found that childhood television viewing patterns were a better predictor of later aggression than social class, parents' behavior, child rearing practices, and many other measured variables included in the study.

In 1990 George Comstock and Hae-Jung Paik analyzed the results of over 1000 comparisons derived from 185 different experiments and studies using the most advanced methods of statistical analysis. They concluded, "The data of the past decade-and-a-half strengthens rather than weakens the case that television violence increases aggressive and antisocial behavior."

> *"In our urban centers an average family views 77 hours per week."*

In March 1992, Dr. Leonard D. Eron gave testimony before the Senate Committee on Governmental Affairs on the subject of youth violence prevention. Speaking on behalf of the American Psychological Association, Dr. Eron's testimony was unequivocal: "There can no longer be any doubt that heavy exposure to televised violence is one of the causes of aggressive behavior, crime, and violence in society."

Television violence is a matter of serious concern in the international community. Many countries grounded in basic liberties—including Canada, Great Britain, South Africa, Belgium, Finland, Australia, New Zealand, and France, have taken action to combat the problem of television violence—the French government fined two television companies more than 10 million francs for broadcasting excessively violent programs during children's viewing hours.

Australia's Broadcasting Tribunal recommended that broadcasters comply with a code of conduct to be drawn up by the industry with extensive input from the Tribunal and public interest groups. It also recommended that compliance with this code be evaluated when broadcasters attempt to renew their licenses.

New Zealand's Broadcasting Standards Authority has developed detailed regulations on the broadcast of violent images on television. The British Broadcasting Corporation has also developed guidelines relating to the depiction of violence on television. As of January 1994, a tough new broadcasters' code to control television violence, backed up by the Canadian FCC, went into effect in Canada.

Given the overwhelming consensus in the scientific community that television violence is harmful, and the failure of the television industry to regulate itself, the Federal Communications Commission's duty to safeguard the public interest strongly suggests that the FCC should issue carefully crafted rules in order to protect children from television violence.

Set of Rules Urged on TV Violence

On March 25, 1993, the National Foundation to Improve Television filed a Petition for Rule Making with the FCC proposing that the FCC issue a set of rules concerning dramatized violence in television programming. These rules would require telecasters to:

1. Do not telecast programming containing an excessive amount of dramatized violence between 6:00 a.m. and 10:00 p.m.
2. Provide explicit viewer advisories for programming containing an excessive amount of dramatized violence telecast between 6:00 a.m. and 10:00 p.m.
3. Superimpose visual warning signals on programming containing amounts of dramatized violence inappropriate for children telecast between the hours of 6:00 a.m. and 10:00 p.m.
4. Do not transmit promotions or advertisements for programming telecast between 6:00 a.m. and 10:00 p.m., which promotions or advertisements contain an excessive amount of violence.
5. Develop a standard scheme for classifying television programming (a program rating system) on the basis of the amount of dramatized violence it contains.
6. Educate and inform children about the harmful effects of violence, and educate and inform viewers about the harmful effects of exposure to television violence.
7. When showing programming containing dramatized violence between 6:00 a.m. and 10:00 p.m., follow general guidelines to be developed by the FCC in consultation with the television industry.

To date, the FCC has done nothing with respect to this petition even though a broad coalition of national organizations, including the PTA, National Council of Churches, and the American Medical Association, now support the adoption of these measures. If such inaction continues, the National Foundation to Improve Television will ask the Federal Court of Appeals to require the FCC to take action. . . .

First Amendment Questions

Developments in First Amendment case law indicate that carefully drawn rules on television violence, such as those proposed in the National Foundation to Improve Television's Petition to the FCC, would not violate the free speech rights of television broadcasters or cable operators.

In 1979 a federal court recognized that scientific evidence of the danger posed by televised violence might someday justify increased governmental regulation of television programming. The *Zamora* court denied recovery of tort damages from broadcasters for a murder committed by a boy who watched an extremely high amount of televised violence on the ground that imposing civil liability in such a case would violate the First Amendment. However, the *Zamora* court also noted, "One day, medical or other sciences with or without the cooperation of programmers may convince the FCC or the Courts that the delicate balance of First Amendment rights

> *"Television violence is a matter of serious concern in the international community."*

should be altered to permit some additional limitations in programming."

District of Columbia Federal Judge Edwards's citation of a television violence study in his concurring opinion in a November 1993 case suggests that we now have exactly the sort of evidence foreseen in 1979 by the *Zamora* court. Judge Edwards notes that the scientific evidence supporting regulation of violent programming is compelling, but that such evidence is lacking with respect to indecent programming: "The apparent lack of specific evidence of harms from indecent programming stands in direct contrast, for example, to the evidence of harm caused by violent programming—a genre that, as yet, has gone virtually unregulated."

To evaluate whether exposure to television violence is a cause of societal violence, University of Washington researcher Brandon Centerwall compared the homicide rates of the United States and Canada to that of South Africa, where an affluent, Westernized white population remained without television until 1975. In a study published in *JAMA* (the *Journal of the American Medical Association*), Centerwall showed that homicide rates among white Americans nearly doubled between the introduction of television in the 1950's and 1975. The biggest surge came after 1965, just as the first television generation reached adolescence.

Centerwall found that age distribution, urbanization, economic conditions, alcohol consumption, capital punishment, civil unrest, and the availability of firearms could not account for the increase. In the case of

> *"The FCC should issue carefully crafted rules in order to protect children from television violence."*

South Africa, the homicide figures remained flat for the years the country was without television, between 1950 and 1975. But in 1987, the first South African television generation had come of age, and South Africa's homicide rate had more than doubled in 12 years. Centerwall concludes, "[I]f, hypothetically, television technology had never been developed, there would today be 10,000 fewer homicides each year in the United States, 70,000 fewer rapes, and 700,000 fewer injurious assaults."

Regulatory Attention Deserved

The Centerwall article is only one of the many hundreds of studies that strongly suggest excessive amounts of dramatized violence in television programming are at least as deserving of regulatory attention as indecent language broadcast into the home by radio or excessively loud rock music in a city park. Now that television violence is known to be harmful, we must seriously question whether the television industry can be relied upon to reduce voluntarily the amount of violence on television to safe levels.

Although the television networks did declare their adoption of viewer advisories, the advisories have been spotty and of little real help to parents because the warnings are not given in the newspaper television schedules. The warnings are contemporaneous rather than being in advance, so the advisory really provides no warning at all.

Similarly, the broadcast networks have refused to support a program-rating system, thus rendering blind any computer chip on a television set (as proposed by Massachusetts Congressman Edward J. Markey's Telecommunications Committee) that would allow a parent to block out violent-rated programming. The broadcasters' position is indefensible since such a computer chip is the ultimate parental empowerment parents can use once and for all to protect their children from unwelcome fictional violent programming.

Given this stubborn resistance of the industry to reform itself, it appears that we have no alternative but to ask the FCC to take action.

In addition to supporting governmental action to reduce violence on television, those interested in improving television can encourage broadcasters and cable operators to make good on their promises through phone calls, letters and visits to station offices. They should write letters to offending stations and advertisers who support violent programming.

> *"Carefully drawn rules on television violence . . . would not violate the free speech rights of television broadcasters."*

While recent legal developments show that regulating television violence is permissible under the First Amendment, recent history suggests that the government will not take action, and broadcasters will not regulate themselves, unless concerned citizens make their voices heard. Organizations such as the National Foundation to Improve Television are working hard to reduce the amount of violence on television, but public opinion is what really counts with the government, broadcasters, cable operators, and advertisers.

Public opinion polls suggest that approximately 80 percent of Americans think television is too violent. If a similar percentage of people would only make their views known directly to the FCC, Congress, stations and advertisers, through letters, phone calls and other means, we could finally expect to see a long-overdue reduction in violent television programming. There is no question that our children would be the better for it.

Boycotts of Advertisers Could Reduce Media Violence

by Daniel Schorr

About the author: *Daniel Schorr, a noted journalist for many years, is senior news analyst for National Public Radio.*

I had 23 rewarding years with CBS News as a correspondent at home and abroad and six years with Ted Turner and CNN. And if both associations ended with blow-ups over what I considered issues of principle, I harbor no hard feelings.

Television Promotes Violence

My problem with television goes beyond my own relations with the medium, although my experience in television gave me a special sensitivity to its baneful effects on the American psyche. Let me put it in a sound-bite: Television, celebrating violence, promotes violence. By rewarding terrorism, it encourages terrorism. By trivializing great issues, it buries great issues. By blurring the line between fantasy and reality, it crowds our reality. And people are beginning to catch on.

I do not know why conservatives seem generally more concerned about sex on television and liberals more concerned about violence on television. The Christian right is appalled at the number of sex scenes. Of 45 such scenes watched by USA Today in a sample week, only 4 involved married couples. Thirty-nine involved adulterers or unmarried persons.

Others are more appalled by violence. By the age of 18, according to the National Coalition on Television Violence, the average American will have witnessed 200,000 acts of violence, including 40,000 murders. Opinion polls indicate that up to 80 percent of Americans today think there is too much violence on television.

Daniel Schorr, "TV Violence—What We Know but Ignore," *The Christian Science Monitor*, September 7, 1993. Reprinted with permission.

"In the absence of family, peer, and school relationships," said the 1969 National Commission on Violence, "television becomes the most compatible substitute for real life experience." John Hinckley, who withdrew from school and family life, spent many hours alone in a room with a TV set, retreating into a world of fantasy violence. When questioned by the Secret Service after shooting President Reagan in 1981, he first asked, "Is it on TV?" Anyone who has worked in television knows of its power to create a reality of its own that may crowd our *real* reality.

Televised Terror

Less benign is what people will sometimes do to get themselves and their causes authenticated by television. Prison rioters sometimes list as a primary demand that they be able to air their grievances on television. You may say that TV is the victim, not the instigator of terrorism. But the dirty little secret is that television enjoys the tingle of a terrorist incident. It enjoys the ratings, and profits, that go with televised terror. ABC scored an exclusive interview with the captain of a hijacked TWA plane in Lebanon, who spoke with a captor's gun to his head. A triumph for ABC—and a triumph for the terrorists who gained international recognition by this promotional stunt.

"Television, celebrating violence, promotes violence."

NBC had an exclusive interview with Abu Abass, wanted for murder in the hijacking of the cruise ship *Achille Lauro*, and NBC agreed not to reveal where it had interviewed the fugitive, who used his opportunity to justify terrorism on American TV. Anthony Quainton, who used to head the State Department's Office for Combatting Terrorism, has associated the increase in casualties during hijackings and hostage-takings during the 1980s with a desire to ensure media attention.

Channel 7 in Miami, long at the bottom of the ratings pile, has emerged as one of the most successful independent stations in the nation. Why? On a typical evening, Channel 7 reported on three rapes, two plane crashes, three hit-and-run accidents, and a wild-monkey attack.

The quest for ratings is not limited to the entertainment studio. It has spread to the newsroom—in case you can still tell the difference. The "docu-drama," and, more recently, the syndicated "reality-based shows," as they are called, have almost erased the line between fact and fiction. News programmers are sometimes driven to recreation themselves.

In 1989, the *ABC Evening News* showed a simulation, not immediately identified as such, of an American diplomat suspected of espionage handing over a briefcase full of secrets to a Russian agent.

I suspect that kids who go around shooting kids, on purpose or at random, no longer know the difference between the bang-bang they grow up with on the television screen and the bang-bang that snuffs out real lives. Maybe the kids they shoot will come back to life after the commercial. The desensitizing effect of endless violent acts is the most destructive aspect of television's general assault on a sense of reality. E.B. White predicted in the 1940s that television would become either "the test of the modern world, a saving radiance," or "a new and unbearable disturbance of the modern peace." Which is it?

Violence and sex on television have not developed by happenstance. In the 1950s, ABC, the youngest and least watched of the three networks, found a formula to catch up with NBC and CBS. It was *The Untouchables*, a program full of violence, highly successful, that established murder and mayhem as the way to lift ratings. Script writers today will tell you that they are ordered to insert more scenes of sex and violence and that scripts have been rejected for being too tame.

"The most important thing," said former U.S. Surgeon General Jesse Steinfeld in 1972, "is that a causal relationship has been shown between violence-viewing and aggression." The Commission on Violence and Youth of the American Psychological Association reported 5 to 6 violent acts per hour on prime time, 20 to 25 on Saturday morning children's programs. Cable and MTV had more. Finding: "There is absolutely no doubt that higher levels of viewing on television are correlated with increased acceptance of aggressive attitudes and increased aggressive behavior. . . . Children's exposure to violence in the mass media, particularly at young ages, can have harmful lifelong consequences."

TV's Cover-Up

We have long known all this. The media have often covered up such knowledge. In 1968 CBS assigned me to cover the hearings of the National Commission on the Causes and Prevention of Violence, after the assassination of Martin Luther King Jr. and Robert Kennedy.

One interim report dealt with TV and violence. I taped a summary for the *Evening News*. Shortly before air time I was told that CBS executives had intervened to censor my report. One item deleted was a paragraph stating that while "most persons will not kill after seeing a single violent television program . . . it is possible that many learn some of their attitudes about violence." My protest almost got me fired.

But TV can no longer hide its love affair with violence. The networks, feeling the heat and fearing federal intervention, now offer warning labels. But for the quarter of American families that are now single-parent families, the parent is usually at work. Who is there to exercise discretion? Isn't the warning actually bait for kids?

> *"The quest for ratings . . . has spread to the newsroom."*

Congress has been looking at the problem of television and violence since 1952, and now there is some sentiment in Congress to control violence by legislation. One bill would mandate a chip enabling viewers to block out programs that the networks classify as violent. Networks are reluctant to put the label on for the obvious reason that advertisers will stay away from such programs. Rep. John Bryant (D) of Texas has a bill that says: Cut violence or you will be fined,

> *"TV can no longer hide its love affair with violence."*

and stations may lose licenses when they come up for renewal. In a Senate hearing, Sen. Howard Metzenbaum (D) of Ohio told network executives, "Do something or else."

This raises First Amendment issues. The courts hold that a regulated industry, using channels that really belong to the public, cannot escape regulation. But any move to regulate for contents stirs profound unease in a supporter of free speech and free press. Nothing is more likely to bring on a threat to the First Amendment than abuse of the First Amendment. By law, after all, television is supposed to operate "in the public interest, convenience, and necessity."

Why is it so hard to get television to control its love affair with violence? Because of perverse economic incentives. Because violence sells. Why does it sell? Because the public buys it. We all make the violence profitable.

I like Attorney General Janet Reno's recommendation that parents refuse to buy products that advertise on violent television programs. Does that sound like "boycott"? Yes. But the problem of violence on television will not be resolved until economic incentives are reversed. Organized public action will be more effective than government regulation.

As for E.B. White's choice between "saving radiance" or "unbearable disturbance": We've had the disturbance. We wait for the saving radiance.

High-Tech TV Locks Could Reduce the Negative Impact of Media Violence

by Amitai Etzioni

About the author: *Amitai Etzioni, a leading spokesperson for the communitarian movement, is the author of the book* The Spirit of Community *and the editor of the quarterly* The Responsive Community: Rights and Responsibilities.

The gadget is small: it can easily be incorporated into your next TV set. (Or, if you insist, attached to your old one.) By punching in a few numbers, you can ensure that your child will never see another violent show on your home TV set. The issue at hand, however, is far from small. Nothing less is at stake than the question of whether a community may edit its culture, or whether it must be subject to limitless gore and filth so as not to curb anyone's right to express himself and make money.

Past Errors

Until recently there was less than a broad consensus that television violence is a problem in need of treatment. On the contrary, while conservatives railed against pornography (sometimes in an uneasy alliance with feminists), liberals insisted that we have no business regulating show business. While these liberals did bemoan the spread of violence in the culture, they had neither the ideas nor the stomach to do anything about it.

Moreover, the social sciences, which act as a kind of semi-independent source of facts and observations, offered no further illumination. I hate to admit it, but over a lifetime of teaching sociology, I too tended to follow the dictates of the social sciences. Violence in the media was harmless, went the textbook mantra; there was no evidence of any "correlation" between exposure to violence (or, for that matter, hard-core porn) and anti-social behavior. On the contrary, social scientists used to opine, expressing violent urges when watching, say, *Fatal At-*

Amitai Etzioni, "Lock Up Your TV Set," *National Review*, October 18, 1993, ©1993 by National Review, Inc., 150 E. 35th St., New York, NY 10016. Reprinted by permission.

traction, The Last Action Hero, or *Lethal Weapon* may vent these feelings in a harmless manner and obviate the need to act them out.

True, there were some incidents that contradicted the social sciences. *Friday the 13th*, a slasher movie, quickly found a live imitator. A movie about violence in the ghetto, *Colors*, led viewers to riot in several cities. A group of black teenagers, incensed over the violence depicted in *Mississippi Burning*, beat a white 14-year-old into unconsciousness.

> *"Media violence is one of the key ingredients in the complex mix of factors that produce anti-social conduct."*

Some media moguls, such as Disney's Michael Eisner, still suggest that movies like *Terminator* release more aggression than they build up. However, by now the social sciences have caught up. There is mounting evidence that violence in the media is one factor that breeds real violence in the body of society.

- A rural Canadian town began receiving TV signals for the first time in 1973, and the rate of violent behavior among young children increased 160 per cent in the following two years. University of British Columbia researchers found that the rate of aggression rose among both boys and girls and was widespread. Two similar towns nearby had had TV for some time and experienced no such increase between 1973 and 1975.

- A University of Illinois at Chicago study found that the amount of television a child watches at age eight predicts the severity of violent acts later committed as an adult. Even after controlling for factors such as intelligence, socioeconomic status, and baseline aggressiveness, the study found that individuals who watched more television as children were more likely to become abusive adults. This statistic becomes particularly alarming when one considers that about half of children six and older have their own TV set in their bedroom.

- A study commissioned by CBS in 1978 found that children who had watched an above-average amount of violence on television before adolescence were, as teenagers, committing acts such as assault, rape, major vandalism, and abuse of animals at a rate 49 per cent higher than those who had experienced little TV violence.

- A Harvard psychologist, Ronald G. Slaby, pointed out that the impact goes beyond increasing aggression. Children also experience a victim effect (increased fearfulness) and a bystander effect (increased callousness and desensitization to violence).

- After the anti–Vietnam War movie *The Deer Hunter* was first shown on national television, with the Russian-roulette scene left intact, some 29 copycat incidents were reported, 26 of which were fatal.

As the body of evidence accumulated and public concern mounted, Congress moved to conduct hearings on the subject. Predictably, media moguls protested that TV should not be blamed for having caused all that violence. Warren Littlefield, president of NBC Entertainment, argued that children are affected by poverty, broken homes, and communities awash with drugs and handguns.

Fair enough. However, even television producers and broadcasters had a hard time denying that media violence is one of the key ingredients in the complex mix of factors that produce anti-social conduct.

Freedom to Self-Destruct

If it was not easy to reach a consensus that there is a problem, it is even more challenging to find an antidote. In part the issue is philosophical. There is a strong sense, at least in the sizable parts of the community influenced by libertarians, that as people must live with the consequences of their acts, they should be free to choose their own poison if they so desire. Thus, if they wish to numb their minds by watching re-runs of *HeeHaw*, it is *their* minds that are deactivated. If they are too busy watching boxing matches on HBO to taste the joys of reading a fine novel, it is *their* lives that are diminished. This argument has less validity when it comes to footage that fosters violent predispositions, the consequences of which others must bear. However, very few see the nexus between watching violent television and acting out as sufficiently binding to justify anything even remotely resembling censorship. (After all, the correlation between possessing handguns and violence is much stronger, and guns are not banned.)

> *"We assist parents in guiding their children when it comes to mild and full-blown porn, but not when it comes to violence."*

The philosophical context changes fundamentally, though, when we turn to minors. Their hearts and minds and willpower are still inchoate. It is an elementary fact that infants are born without any moral or social values. Unless they are provided with the values that the community cherishes, they will grow up to be morally defective adults, if not full-blown psychopaths. After they gain values and mature, youngsters may change their course, even rebel against the community consensus. First, however, they must learn what that consensus is. Learning that violence is not the way to dispose of one's problems is an integral part of the lessons that any civil society must pass on from generation to generation.

Remembering that the community agents in charge of the moral initiation of the young are clearly their parents brings us to the crux of the matter: how to enable them to discharge this duty when it comes to watching television. I stress "enable" because it will not do to preach to parents if the tools they require are not available. Parents cannot shape what values television instills in their children if information about what a TV program contains is not available, or if they have no effective means to enforce their decisions. As a father of five wonderful but not completely perfect sons, let me tell you that standing next to the TV set 24 hours a day is not quite the way to go.

123

It is a rather special American tradition, unlike the Scandinavian one, that we assist parents in guiding their children when it comes to mild and full-blown porn, but not when it comes to violence. Thus, there are R and X ratings for movies, but so far no V ratings. The only things that we cover in brown paper wrappers and sell behind drawn shades are depictions of explicit sex—not decapitation, evisceration, or murder.

Attempting to Prod the Media

In 1993, a few members of Congress decided to prod producers and broadcasters to do to media violence a bit of what they have done to porn. The congressmen knew that they could not pass laws that would survive the media lobby. However, they hoped that hearings on the subject would encourage the media industry, ever publicity conscious, into action. They overestimated what mere prodding can accomplish.

The hearings focused on two bills that had no more chance of being enacted than late-night TV has of being turned over to the University without Walls. One bill, introduced by Representative Edward J. Markey (D., Mass.), proposed that TV shows be rated like movies, and that TV sets be equipped with locks. The other bill, proposed by Senator Byron L. Dorgan (D., N.D.), would have the Federal Communications Commission keep a "violence report card" listing the number of violent acts on television each quarter—which seems to me to introduce a government agency where it is best left out.

The media, in any case, can be a mulish beast. Only Sega of America, a Japanese-based manufacturer of video games, voluntarily offered to rank its products. The rest of the media moguls responded by agreeing to introduce a generic warning—"Due to some violent content, parental discretion advised"— for a trial period of two years. Translation: until the publicity dies down.

For such a warning to be effective, moreover, parents must be present when the program starts. When the parents are absent, they are left with no tool to control their children's TV viewing. Such ratings alone, then, are in reality no more practical than standing guard around the clock. Indeed, warnings could have the opposite of the intended effect: according to Terry Rakolta, founder of Americans for Responsible Television, the warnings may actually attract children to forbidden footage.

Hence the need for a TV lock—actually a chip that reads signals sent over the airwaves. The technology is similar to that now used to transmit

> *"Ratings alone . . . are in reality no more practical than standing guard around the clock."*

closed-caption information to deaf viewers: an unused portion of TV signals can be adapted to tell the chip what is forthcoming. Some critics argue that technically deficient parents will not be able to use a TV lock any more than they are able to set their VCR, and may well have to resort to having their children program the locks! However, this is hardly a serious obstacle. The chips can be made to be as user-friendly as the new VCR-plus. The parent simply punches a number into the lock, setting it at a given violence rating, then protects it from tampering through a simple childproof code, and the chip does the rest.

> *"The fears of censorship are highly exaggerated."*

Others argue that it is difficult to define what constitutes violence; that some shows with a higher body count are less violent than those that feature close-ups of gore—and from there the considerations multiply. Howard Stringer, president of CBS broadcasting group, points to *Julius Caesar* as a film that would fall victim to a V rating, and fears that a violence warning would end the presentation of all drama on TV. Some psychologists warn that *Jurassic Park* may be too "intense" for children; after all, the dinosaurs *eat* people. A *Washington Post* writer was worried about the fate of *Dracula*. Yet the networks already have in-house reviewers who disallow certain scenes; these reviewers could serve on a new industry-wide rating committee.

The Devil Knows Where

Then there is the predictable slippery-slope argument. Lucie Salhany, chairman of Fox Broadcasting, warns that if we have a V chip, all sorts of censorship will follow: "Will we have the sex chip? And what about the news chip?" If you accept this notion, then we never can change the status quo, however perverted, out of fear that the suggested changes may lead us the Devil knows where. However, the fears of censorship are highly exaggerated. Containing our torrential floods of TV violence with a few optional devices is no more likely to stem our freedom of expression than sandbags can dam the Mississippi.

Last but not least, media representatives maintain that they only show what the public wants to see. Jack Valenti, president of the Motion Picture Association of America, puts it like this: "There is one thing movie people worship. It is not ideology, it is not Democratic, it is not Republican. Hollywood worships audiences." If nobody wanted to watch violent movies and tapes, they would self-destruct.

Yet the truth is that the media respond not only to numbers on the bottom line but also to changes in community values—when these are in line with the liberal proclivities of major segments of the media. Thus if you watch a random set of programs you will find black neurosurgeons, judges, and police chiefs in a much higher proportion than their actual presence in the population. In other words, these representations are not demographically but politically correct. When President Ronald Reagan complained about the glorification of drug use in the movies, the industry first denied this was the case—and then mended its ways. Particularly revealing was a moot court organized by Fred Friendly in which several producers and broadcasters participated. All those consulted agreed that they would not produce or show a movie expressing the views of the KKK, whatever the demand. In short, when it suits the media industry, it is quite capable of editing itself.

All that we require now is to ensure that violence is added to the media's checklist of what must be toned down. The media may well find that there are more creative ways of depicting conflict than resorting to the mass butchery of stunt people. However, there is another consideration at work. The media may well refuse to budge on the issue of TV locks for fear that parents will set them to significantly curtail the amount of TV exposure of all kinds rather than just exposure to violence.

Here the public had best turn its message to the producers not of TV tapes, but of TV sets: give us the locks as an option at a reasonable cost. (While they currently cost $96 or more, if mass-produced they may sell for as little as $5 each.) Given a V-rating system and a TV lock, parents can do the rest.

Media Literacy Education Can Effectively Combat Media Violence

by Elizabeth Thoman

About the author: *Elizabeth Thoman is executive director of the Center for Media in Los Angeles and the founder of* Connect *magazine.*

Violence cannot be sanitized out of our culture even if, as I hope, gruesome and gratuitous violence becomes more and more "politically incorrect" in popular entertainment. Over the decades, we've seen the media industry self-censor many negative ideas and images—from the *Amos 'n' Andy* stereotype of African-Americans to the depiction of alcohol, cigarettes and hard drugs as glamorous. There are some things that responsible writers and directors just don't do anymore. Excessive violence should be added to the list.

There will still be violence in the media, as in life, because there is evil in the world and human nature has its shadow side. There is also grinding poverty and substance abuse and meaninglessness that create a seedbed for violence as a way for some to cope with injustice.

The parameters of our public discourse about media and violence are complex. There are 1st Amendment concerns as well as public policies resulting from years of deregulation of the media industry and the erosion of the public-interest standard in favor of marketplace forces.

Violent Myths

As so many observers point out, violence is the stuff of our fundamental mythologies, including the myth of the American West. While Hollywood may feed these myths, it did not start them. Nor can Washington legislate them away. "Parental advisories" may help some, but they are not a solution.

Violence is a major health problem today and we must find workable solutions to prevent its further spread. I believe that media-literacy education must

Elizabeth Thoman, "Use the Mind to Confront Violence," *Los Angeles Times*, July 25, 1993. Reprinted with permission.

be a component of any effective effort at violence prevention, for both individuals and society as a whole.

Media literacy, as defined in a 1992 report from the Aspen Institute, is the movement "to expand notions of literacy to include the powerful post-print media that dominate our informational landscape." In classrooms as well as informal groups such as Scout troops or parenting classes, people of all ages learn to apply a variety of critical-thinking skills to the thousands of images, words and sounds that bombard us daily. Although well-established in other countries, media-literacy education is just beginning in the United States. It's about time.

Media-literacy programs do not excuse the storytellers of society from responsibility for our cultural environment. But here are five ways that effective media-literacy education can contribute to lessening the impact of violence in our lives:

• *Reduce exposure, by educating parents and caregivers.* How many times have you been to a movie rated "R" for violence and seen children there? Adults, especially men whose viewing habits tend toward action-adventure, need to get the message that too much media violence can truly harm children. Parent organizations, churches, libraries and community groups can sponsor media-literacy programs to help parents develop and enforce age-appropriate viewing limits.

• *Change the impact of violent images that are seen.* This can be done by deconstructing the techniques used to stage violent scenes and decoding the various depictions of violence in news, cartoons, drama, sports and music. It is important for children to learn early on the difference between reality and fantasy and to know how costumes, camera angles and special effects can fool them. Media-literacy activities need to be integrated into every learning environment—schools, churches and temples, after-school groups and clubs.

Nonviolent Role Models

• *Explore alternatives to stories that focus on violence as the solution to interpersonal conflict.* Schools and daycare centers, libraries and families need to have collections of books and videos that provide positive role models to help counterbalance the actions and attitudes of today's "superheroes." Through media-literacy classes, parents can also learn to transform undesirable images from popular culture into opportunities for positive modeling. One father, for example, agreed to let his child watch *Teen-Age Mutant Ninja Turtles*, but

> *"There will still be violence in the media, as in life, because there is evil in the world and human nature has its shadow side."*

only if the child would imagine a fifth turtle named "Gandhi." Later, they discussed how "Ninja Gandhi" might get the Turtles out of trouble without violence.

• *Uncover and challenge the cultural, economic and political supports for me-*

dia violence as well as the personal ways we may each be contributing to it. Media-literacy education empowers viewers to make the connections between what they see on the screen and what they experience at home, at work, at school. Media violence is not isolated from other social issues. And we must not forget that the root of our cherished freedom of speech was not the freedom to protect creativity but the freedom to challenge the political and economic status quo.

> *"Media-literacy education must be a component of any effective effort at violence prevention."*

• *Promote informed and rational public debate in schools, community and civic gatherings, religious groups and in the media.* The reality of our current situation demands that we ask ourselves what kind of culture we want our children to grow up in and whether we can continue to allow the media to profit from products that are clearly contributing to a social condition that endangers public safety.

Media Violence Should Be Treated as a Public Health Problem

by Anthea Disney

About the author: *Anthea Disney is the editor in chief of* TV Guide.

Imagine the following label affixed to your television set: Warning—Watching Television May Be Hazardous to Your Children's Health.

If that sounds radical, consider the studies that convincingly demonstrate a correlation between the frequent viewing of violence and aggressive behavior in youngsters.

A study commissioned by *TV Guide* shows that there is more violence entering our homes than ever before. It's coming from many more sources: home video, pay-per-view and cable, as well as from broadcast networks and local stations. The primary offenders are music videos, reality shows, cartoons and promos for violent theatrical movies.

Violence in a Day

In a single, random day of television programming tracked in Washington, D.C., for *TV Guide*, 1,846 individual acts of violence were observed.

(The magazine defined violence as "any deliberate act involving physical force or the use of a weapon in an attempt to achieve a goal, further a cause, stop the action of another, act out an angry impulse, defend oneself from attack, secure a material reward, or intimidate others.")

Our study found:

- Of the programming monitored, cartoons were the most violent category, with 471 violent scenes in just one day.
- 21 percent of all the violence—389 scenes—involved a life-threatening assault; 362 scenes involved gunplay.
- Cable networks averaged three times as much violence as the "Big Three"

Anthea Disney, "Why Not Treat TV Violence as a Public Health Issue?" *TV Guide*, August 22-28, 1992. 1992 copyright, News America Publications, Inc. (*TV Guide* Magazine). Reprinted with permission from *TV Guide*.

commercial networks (ABC, CBS, and NBC). Specifically, music videos proved to be a greater source of televised violence than previously imagined. MTV showed as much violence as the three commercial networks combined.

It has been estimated that by the time a child graduates from elementary school, he or she will have witnessed at least 8,000 murders and more than 100,000 acts of violence on television.

In her book *Deadly Consequences*, Deborah Prothrow-Stith, assistant dean of government and community programs at the Harvard School of Public Health, points out that inner-city children may be more vulnerable to the effects of violence on television.

These kids watch more TV because they spend more time indoors—the streets are dangerous and there are few other recreational choices. They also have fewer male role models countering the TV superhero who's solving problems with violence.

So what can we do, short of censorship but beyond hand-wringing?

Why not treat TV violence as a public health issue, as we do already with cigarette smoking and drunken driving? Think how much those campaigns have changed people's attitudes and behavior and, most important, saved lives.

To take the same approach with TV programming would involve an intensive public education campaign and strenuous encouragement of the television industry to be sensitive to the problem and deglamorize physical force and the people who resort to it.

As Peggy Charren, president of Action for Children's Television, said, "You have to help parents understand that that box in the living room is not always a friend of the family."

Hope for Improved Television

It's up to parents to make the effort to watch what their children are watching so that they can screen out overly violent programs and discuss what the make-believe acts of violence would mean in real life. Kids often don't seem to understand the true repercussions of a violent act; on TV, there frequently are no repercussions.

If the new season reflects TV at its best, episodes on the 1992 Los Angeles riots will illuminate the conditions that led to the violence, not trivialize them and sensationalize the effect in images that may again become reality.

Many programmers and producers do really care about the results of the shows they air. But they live by the "overnights"—the Nielsen ratings, which define a success or a failure in television terms—and under that kind of pressure, the slope from relevance to sensationalism is a slippery one.

But if, through education and the proper treatment by the industry, TV violence becomes viewed as distasteful and inappropriate, hopefully any meaningless violent act will end up with the same inglorious appeal as a drunk killing people on the highway.

A Bipartisan, Moderate Approach to Media Violence Is Needed

by Philip Berroll

About the author: *Philip Berroll is a New York–based playwright.*

> *"I think [there] is an unavoidable civil war culturally about where this country is going."*
>
> —Newt Gingrich

Liberals who thought that the issues of morality and offensiveness in American popular culture had been buried—along with the Republicans who raised them—in the 1992 election had an unpleasant surprise in May 1993 when a Senate Judiciary subcommittee held hearings on the issue of violence on television. After tongue-lashing network executives for excessively violent programming, the lawmakers—including such liberals as Howard Metzenbaum and Paul Simon—threatened greater restrictions on the broadcasting business. "If you do nothing," Metzenbaum predicted, "we are going to come down harder on you than you would like . . . the Senate giveth, and the Senate can take away." Duly chastened, the top officials of CBS, NBC, ABC, and the Fox Network announced plans for an industry-wide summit in Los Angeles to further discuss the issue; fall programming schedules which emphasized "family-oriented" programming; and most loudly trumpeted, a formal agreement to include parental advisory messages before and during particularly violent programming, suggesting that what was being broadcast was unsuitable for children.

Unanswered Questions

But such warnings as "the program you are about to see may contain content objectionable to certain viewers . . ." already appear at the beginning of many "adult" (i.e. sexually) oriented TV shows, and they are generally regarded as little more than a fig-leaf, face-saving gesture by which broadcasters can demon-

Philip Berroll, "Cultural Elites, Closet Values." Reprinted from TIKKUN MAGAZINE: A BI-MONTHLY JEWISH CRITIQUE OF POLITICS, CULTURE, AND SOCIETY (September/October 1993). Subscriptions are $31.00 per year from TIKKUN, 251 W. 100th St., 5th Floor, New York, NY 10025.

strate "responsibility" while avoiding the really tough decisions about what to broadcast. The new advisory messages would appear to have little more effect; furthermore, independent local stations and cable networks are not even party to the agreement. Meanwhile, the larger questions—what constitutes "offensive" art and entertainment, and whether it should be censored or restricted in any way—remain unanswered.

> *"Those who produce the popular art of America . . . are out of touch with the sensibilities of the average citizen."*

The "offensiveness issue" has clearly outlasted the change of administrations [from Ronald Reagan and George Bush to Bill Clinton] and the end of the conservative, Republican hegemony. Shortly after his presidential victory, Bill Clinton was quoted in *TV Guide* as being "mortified" by many current films and television programs, calling for the entertainment industry to start "deglamorizing mindless sex and violence." And a recent American Psychological Association report, *Big World, Small Screen*, building on the results of earlier studies, concluded that "accumulated research clearly demonstrates a correlation between viewing violence and aggressive behavior—that is, heavy viewers behave more aggressively than light viewers."

Listen to the Message

In truth, the persistence of this issue in the national consciousness should not surprise anyone. In June of 1992—at the time of then–Vice President Dan Quayle's attack on Murphy Brown [an unwed pregnant character on a TV show] and "the cultural elite"—Kenneth L. Woodward wrote in *Newsweek* that "in fixing national attention on the dubious products of the popular media, Quayle has chosen the one aspect of American culture about which everyone has a gripe"; he cited a poll taken by the magazine in which 49 percent of the respondents believed that television entertainment had a negative effect on children, and 80 percent felt that movies contained too much violence and sex. Woodward was one of several commentators who suggested that much as we might want to dismiss the messenger, the message was worth noting: that there really *was* something to the charge that those who produce the popular art of America (be they located in Hollywood, Rockefeller Center, or the lofts and galleries of Soho) are out of touch with the sensibilities of the average citizen and often go out of their way to offend those sensibilities.

The debate over freedom of expression and censorship of material deemed offensive has special significance for American progressives, for whom it represents another fault line with many people who might otherwise share their perspective on economic and other quality-of-life questions. Many Americans continue to believe that liberals do not share or are actively hostile toward their concerns about what comes out of their radios and across their TV and movie screens. In the words of conservative political analyst Kevin Phillips, ". . . there are (non-economic) aspects of ordinary Americans' frustration . . . that liberals and Democrats ignore or sidestep. This is the frequent dishonesty of left-wing populism"; and one such aspect, clearly, is the state of American popular culture. Why is this so? Because with few exceptions, the thought and action of many progressives in these matters has been self-righteously dogmatic and, at the same time, riddled with inconsistencies (which they continually fail to acknowledge). And if we are to have any hope of removing the culture weapon from the Right's political arsenal, this has to change. For a start, we must take a long, hard look at some of our most cherished beliefs in this area.

An Absolute Good

The basic liberal position on the subject begins with the premise that censorship is bad—dangerous to creativity, imagination, and the free exchange of ideas. Although they will, unless they are First Amendment absolutists, allow for occasional exceptions (e.g., libel laws, or the Supreme Court decision allowing localities to restrict pornography based on "community standards"), liberals otherwise believe that the right to free expression is an absolute good.

> *"The good liberal will not admit to being personally offended by anything."*

But this philosophy took root in the days when there was real censorship in this country being applied to the likes of Lenny Bruce or the Smothers Brothers (or earlier, to literary figures such as James Joyce and Henry Miller). The defenders of free expression perhaps could not have anticipated the sleazy depths of current television programming, the misogyny and violence of the lyrics and personae of certain pop music performers, or the cinematic blood-fests of Stallone and Schwarzenegger—that is, cultural phenomena that might offend *liberals*. Liberals nevertheless are still uncomfortable with the ideas of "offensiveness," or "tastefulness," or "redeeming social value," believing that acknowledging the validity of these concerns might serve the agenda of repressive conservatives. So the good liberal will not admit to being personally offended by anything (even when that is clearly the case), or will insist, "that's not the issue."

But this "censorship is the only question" mentality on the part of most liberals has led to at least three sorts of intellectual dishonesty: First, the labeling as "pro-censorship" of those who raise legitimate objections to various forms of pop culture; second, the refusal even to entertain those objections (such people are dismissed as judgmental, inhibited, "trying to impose their values on others"); and third, the unwillingness to acknowledge their own advocacy of what they would call "regulation" of art and entertainment which they find objectionable. These hypocrisies feed the conservative's caricature of the elitist, double-standard liberal, out of touch with mainstream America.

When "Second Lady" Tipper Gore launched her Parents' Music Resource Center (PMRC) in 1988, she became a villain to the arts community, pilloried in the alternative press as an ally of Senator Jesse Helms, parodied on *Saturday Night Live* (in a sketch in which Satan was a congressional witness). But her actual proposal—the labeling of certain recordings as potentially offensive—was no more restrictive than the movie ratings system or TV's warnings of "adult" content. Even record producer Danny Goldberg, who organized a group to combat the PMRC, has since conceded that Tipper Gore "kept her word" about not favoring actual censorship. (Indeed, after her return to the national spotlight [when her husband was elected vice president], Mrs. Gore pointedly refused to jump on the rap-censorship bandwagon, even though one of the songs on Ice-T's *Body Count* album referred to forcible sex with two of her nieces.)

Parental Worries

Yet these realities have gone largely unacknowledged by Tipper Gore's critics, and some have continued to lampoon her. (Recently, Oliver Stone was quoted as quipping, "Is Tipper Gore going to be our cultural commissar?") Her original motivation—her fears as a parent, rather than her threats as a potential censor—are rarely if ever taken into account. The title of her 1988 book, *Raising PG Kids in an X-Rated Society*, may sound hyperbolic, but it expresses her basic concern: How does an involved parent monitor the media stimuli with which her children, whose critical faculties are yet undeveloped, are bombarded every day? As Nicholas Von Hoffman has written: "Corporate mass media [asserts that] parents . . . should police the TV, they should make sure the children are preserved from the subversion sold in the movie theaters and at the record store. That's fine in an era where both parents work, isn't it?" (Indeed, this is another reason why parental advisories about TV violence could have only a limited effect: If the parents aren't home to see the advisories, what difference would they make?)

Similar worries were voiced by Terry Rakolta, a Michigan mother who was so incensed at the vulgarity of the Fox sitcom *Married . . . with Children* that she attempted to organize a boycott of the show's sponsors. Again, the initial reaction among liberals was to condemn her as a narrow-minded, intolerant prig—there was even a *Murphy Brown* episode featuring a Rakolta caricature.

> *"A boycott is both a legitimate and a very effective form of political expression."*

But while we can argue that it would have been preferable for her to exercise "the censorship of the wrist" by changing channels or turning off her TV, the fact remains that in a capitalist democracy, a boycott is both a legitimate and a very effective form of political expression. (To accuse Rakolta of trying to censor free speech is as unfair as attacking Martin Luther King Jr. and other civil rights leaders who used the boycott weapon for interfering with "free enterprise.") Those who disagree with such boycotts can either exert counter-pressure on sponsors or networks, or open a dialogue with the boycotters to address their concerns.

How many liberals, I wonder, have actually examined the offending material? *Married . . . with Children* features a husband who prefers masturbation to marital sex; his wife, a trampy, lacquer-haired slob; and their weasely son and school-slut daughter, all of whom spend most of each episode insulting or scheming against each other. The show's creators have defended the program as a healthy antidote to the phony harmony of traditional family comedies on TV. I have news

> *"[Liberals], too, have advocated restrictions on media that they have found offensive."*

for them—*Ozzie and Harriet* has been off the air for a quarter-century; and in any event, when it comes to shows about imperfect families, there is more insight and wit in ten minutes of *Roseanne* or even *The Simpsons* than in a month's worth of *Married . . . with Children*. The dominant qualities of *Married . . . with Children* are its sheer stupidity (when all else fails, throw in a witticism from a talking dog) and hypocrisy (in this supposedly vulgarian household, absolutely no one ever says "fuck" either in the literal sense or as punctuation).

One Brush

Lest readers respond with "That's not the issue," let me reiterate: My point in both these cases is that while low quality in itself is certainly not an excuse for censorship, people who object to low quality (or, if you will, trash and sleaze) need not be automatically condemned as would-be censors, nor should their objections be rejected out of hand—sometimes, they could be valid. But many liberals will not acknowledge this possibility; they will insist on smearing all those who disagree with the same "totalitarian" brush, as if there is no distinction between a Tipper Gore and a Donald Wildmon (a strongly conservative Christian activist).

A similar blinkered mentality—and again, exaggerated accusations of censorship—was evident in the brouhaha during the Bush administration over the choice of grant recipients by the National Endowment for the Arts (NEA). Certainly, it was proper and necessary to resist the Right's campaign to turn the endowment into a political football. But one does not have to be an ally of Jesse Helms and his cohorts to be skeptical about their opponents' arguments.

Many if not all of the NEA's critics repeatedly emphasized that money, not censorship, was the issue; they were not advocating that the work of Robert Mapplethorpe be obliterated or that performers such as Karen Finley be silenced, only that tax dollars not be used to subsidize their art. The liberal response was first, to point out that virtually all Americans can find something toward which they do not want their taxes to go (if I can pay for nuclear warheads, you can pay for a crucifix immersed in urine), which is true enough, but amounts to a "two wrongs make a right" defense; and second, to insist that artists have a *right* to governmental support—the denial of that support, therefore, would be tantamount to censorship.

But is the loss of a potential sum of several thousand dollars (before taxes, I presume) really the equivalent of being thrown in jail, having your work burned, or living under an international death sentence? And what about all the artists who draw financial support from teaching, working in a factory, driving a cab—are they somehow less free to express themselves? The critic Eric Bentley, a long-time champion of the avant-garde, put it in perspective:

> Many people came forward to say, "nothing but the merits, purely aesthetic qualities should be considered," which I didn't think was so. I think it's absolutely valid for anyone involved in any way, such as a senator, to express a moral objection when he considers himself morally offended. . . . It's not so surprising that the officers of the government wouldn't like what the younger generation is doing and don't want to put money into it. What's all the bother about? Make a living some other way. I don't think we should become dependent on government subsidy."

The liberal defense of Mapplethorpe, in particular, went beyond the insistence that his offensiveness was not the issue; his advocates would not even acknowledge such offensiveness—they tried to characterize his photographs as positively uplifting, praising the "beauty" of his images, or portraying him as a champion of sexual minorities. Even one of his most passionate defenders, Camille Paglia, rejected

> *"If we believe that some values . . . are better than others, we should not be reluctant to see them expressed."*

that idea. In her view, Mapplethorpe's work is worth defending for what it is— grim, ugly, corrosive—and to pretend otherwise is ridiculous; she decried "the intrusion of strident liberal politics into the assessment of Mapplethorpe. . . . It injures Mapplethorpe to whitewash him, to deny his cunningly perverse motives, to turn him into a gay Norman Rockwell." Apologists for Mapplethorpe who took this tack persuaded no one; their opponents felt patronized, their allies uncomfortable.

Liberals Have Advocated Speech Restrictions

But perhaps the clearest demonstration of liberal "bad faith" thinking on censorship is the denial that they, too, have advocated restrictions on media that they have found offensive, or that they could ever conceive of doing so. Yet how else could one characterize the efforts of Peggy Charren and Action for Children's Television? Mrs. Charren's decades-long campaign, pressuring Congress and the Federal Communications Commission to limit the violent content and commercial messages of Saturday-morning cartoons on TV, was deemed admirable by most progressives, myself included. But let's be clear: In the literal sense, what she was advocating was a limitation on the "free speech" of the producers, networks, and sponsors involved—unlike Terry Rakolta, who never suggested that the government clamp down on Fox. (Mrs. Charren, by the way, has dismissed the networks' parental-advisory plan as "a benign solution, but . . . inadequate.") So there is some justification to the anti-regulation argument voiced in this case by free-market conservatives (although not, of course, by their allies on the religious Right, who have no great qualms about censorship). One could respond with the Marxist assertion that free speech, in a capitalist society, is an illusion—what is produced by Von Hoffman's "corporate mass media" is bought and paid for by the ruling economic interests. But even if this were true, I would reject it on the grounds that it opens up a Pandora's box of potential counter-censorship. (A leftist regime could muzzle anyone on the grounds of being "a stooge of the ruling class"—as often happened back in the USSR.) More to the point, few liberals these days are Marxists. Their failing is that they do not take the free-speech argument seriously in this case simply because this is speech that they do not like. (To take another hypothetical example: What do you think would be the reaction if Fox's *In Living Color*, already notorious for its caricatures of Black homosexuals, started going after Jews?)

So is it a contradiction for liberals to acknowledge exceptions to the rule of across-the-board free speech? I don't believe so—not when the exceptions I mentioned earlier already exist. In any case, in the current situation, it is usually not a matter of calling for restrictions, but to recognize the distinction between objecting to popular art forms—even attacking them—and advocating that they be silenced. We have to remember that the first does not imply the second.

Supporting Values

The challenge for the Left, then, is to readjust its way of thinking—first, by acknowledging its own "closet values" and dropping the pretense of moral neutrality. While we have the right, even the duty, to oppose the imposition of a single set of values on American popular culture, that does not mean that the discussion of values in general is a bad thing; and if we believe that some values (tolerance, non-violence, equality, etc.) *are* better than others, we should not be reluctant to see them expressed.

A few possible ways of putting this into practice come to mind. We can organize "counter-NEAs"—non-governmental funding groups for unconventional artists, which would re-

> *"We should be unafraid to engage in moral criticism of some of our supposed allies."*

move them from the realm of political pressure; we can help schools and religious and community groups to develop "How to Talk Back to Your TV" workshops, showing students how to be discriminating, skeptical viewers of all forms of programming—news, entertainment, and commercials; and we can support the establishment of grant programs similar to that of the American Film Institute for independent filmmakers, enabling them to work outside of Hollywood and its mass-appeal bias.

In response to the Marxists, all of this could be a counterweight to the influence of entrenched economic interests in popular culture. In response to the free-marketeers who claim that the media are simply giving people what they want, I would argue that in truth, they are actively shaping their audience's tastes (if you feed someone an exclusive diet of Spam for years, then Spam is what they will come to prefer), and thus it is worthwhile to give that audience some healthy alternatives from which to choose. (And as for those who argue that this is unnecessary because there is already plenty of "diversity" in our culture, let me remind them that not everyone lives in cities with "art house" movie theaters or gets two dozen channels on TV.)

> *"One can favor absolute free speech 'and still be appalled at the content of the speech that is freely being presented today.'"*

Most of all, we should be unafraid to engage in moral criticism of some of our supposed allies—particularly the Hollywood "creative community," and not just the easily disdainable network and studio bigwigs but also the writers, actors, and directors who do the actual creating. The affinity felt by many progressives toward this group (even when they turn up their noses at its products) is understandable, because its members seem like "our kind of people" in so many ways: They give buckets of money to the " right" causes and candidates, and they are nonjudgmental about individual behavior. But much of this reflects their lifestyle, not their ideology. (According to the *Village Voice*, *Murphy Brown* creator Diane English "runs a production company that is nonunion and offers no health care benefits to most of its employees.") And it has almost nothing to do with what they produce—so much of which is driven by the traditional lowest-common-denominator mentality of American showbiz. Thus the emphasis on gratuitous violence, sex without emotional commitment, a disdain for education and the intellect, quick and painless solutions to complex problems, and the "values" (looks, money, celebrity) of *People* magazine and *Entertainment Tonight*.

Schizophrenic Hollywood

We should have no reluctance about calling our Hollywood "friends" to account for this gap between their professed ideals and their actual creative output. "We all know they're good citizens," says former network boss Grant Tinker, "(but) on the lot, they make creative decisions for the wrong reason(s) . . . They are schizophrenics." The actor Ron Silver, for example, has compiled an admirable record of political activism over the years; but I would like to hear him defend *Blue Steel*, in which he played a crazed yuppie who runs around

Manhattan shooting people, for no other reason than that he enjoys it, until female cop Jamie Lee Curtis guns him down. It is not enough to call such a film—or *Basic Instinct*, or *Lethal Weapon*—"escapist entertainment," with no connection to the society in which it takes place. As Alan Dershowitz put it in an interview, one can favor absolute free speech "and still be appalled at the content of the speech that is freely being presented today."

Finally, when future controversies arise, we can also reject appeals for sanctions from politically correct dogmatists on the Left—while still refusing to be silent in the name of "free expression." I would agree, for instance, with the position of Roger Rosenblatt regarding Bret Ellis's violent, misogynistic novel *American Psycho*. Writing in the *New York Times Book Review* in December 1990, he did not endorse using the boycott weapon (which had been called for by some feminist groups) against Ellis's publishers, but he did ridicule the book and urge readers—prepublication—not to buy it. This put him at odds with John Irving, who argued in a later *Book Review* that "if you slam a book when it's published, that's called book reviewing, (but) three months in advance . . . your intentions are more censorial than critical"—even though Irving himself admitted that "I may identify with Mr. Rosenblatt's literary taste." Rosenblatt responded, "(H)e chooses to interpret my harshness as censorship, while I assume he deems his opinion taste because it is tepidly expressed."

> *"What progressives have to do is to refuse to join the herd mentality of either side."*

It would appear that Senator Simon and Massachusetts Congressman Edward J. Markey, the chief brokers of the television networks' parental-warning agreement, were thinking along those lines—trying to find a happy medium between censorship and the current situation of blood-soaked anarchy. And I think they have succeeded—but only in the most narrowly legalistic sense. The underlying issue has hardly been settled, and perhaps it can never be. Not when the next "hot" young filmmaker, with or without sincere artistic ambitions, will be encouraged to pour on the carnage and vulgarity in his work; when that work will be championed by serious critics, do well at the box office, and eventually be broadcast either on network (with minimal cuts) or cable TV (without any); and when it will then be available to innumerable future audiences through reruns or on cassette. The argument will go on.

Defending Values and Free Expression

What progressives have to do is to refuse to join the herd mentality of either side—to reject both supporters of censorship as the first and best option and the laissez-faire advocates of art for art's—or money's—sake. Let us raise a loud voice in defense of free expression and equally for all other humanistic values; and when the former is used to negate the latter, let us not be afraid to object.

I realize that for the Phyllis Schlaflys [founder of the conservative Eagle Forum] and Donald Wildmons of the world, that will not be enough. Some people will see "perversion" in a picture of two men holding hands, or "blasphemy" in Martin Scorsese's *The Last Temptation of Christ*—just as a sizable number of voters in 1992 apparently believed that Bush and Quayle were doing a fine job. But for everyone else, the efforts I have outlined could be the beginning of a much-needed, and mutually beneficial, outreach effort and perhaps, of a movement to make some positive changes in American mass culture.

If we can disagree with fellow leftists—those feminists who condemned *American Psycho* and others who wish to ban pornography—while acknowledging the very real pain that motivates them, then surely we can do the same, with citizens of other political stripes, in this area. By refusing to caricature or demonize those with whom we disagree, and admitting that we hold no monopoly on truth or tolerance, we can begin to formulate a more positive response to the offensive art question. If not, then we will face the prospect of our continual alienation from those with whom, otherwise, we would have good reason to make common cause.

Kevin Phillips draws a historical parallel: "(Right-wing) politics . . . could not have succeeded if liberalism—first in Weimar [a pre-Hitler period of political freedom and cultural creativity in Germany], then in the United States since the late 1960's—had not in some respects been a politics of avant-garde cabaret values, mockery of patriotism and enthusiastic trespass on bourgeois culture."

I am not suggesting that Dan Quayle, Newt Gingrich, and their friends share the Nazis' sweeping definition of "degenerate art," but their basic attitudes are disturbingly similar. However, if our only response is "if you've got a problem with this, you must be an uptight prude," then we will be adding to their stockpile of political ammunition for decades to come.

A Variety of Measures Could Combat Media Violence

by Suzanne Braun Levine

About the author: *Suzanne Braun Levine is editor of the* Columbia Journalism Review *and editor emerita of* Ms. *magazine.*

I am very proud of the fact that I have never (well, hardly ever) actually sent my kids off to watch TV just to get them out of my hair. I'm less proud of the fact that I don't exert very strong controls over what they watch; and there have even been times when I have caught an image of a horrendous act of violence out of the corner of my eye . . . and kept walking. When they were little, they were content to mellow out over endless reruns of *Mister Rogers' Neighborhood*, but as they got older—they are now eight and ten—and once we acquired a remote control, they began to graze around the dial and learned to snap back to something safe at the sound of an approaching adult.

Hours vs. Content

I do try to limit the number of hours they watch, and I'm pretty good at enforcing the no-TV-before-homework rule; overall my children certainly watch less than the national average of three and a half hours a day. (That is probably due as much to full-time child care as to my moral authority. Parents caught between the demands of a workday and the obscenely outdated 3:00 P.M. school dismissal time have every reason to argue that watching TV—any kind of TV—is preferable to most of the alternatives.) But I must confess it makes me tired just to achieve that level of control; so when it comes to restricting content, I don't always have it in me to take on the philosophical questions of why violence is bad (because it rarely solves anything; because innocent people get hurt; because it is damaging to the soul) and why violence on TV is also bad, but in a different way (because by making it entertaining, TV shows trivialize

Suzanne Braun Levine, "Caution: Children Watching," *Ms.*, July/August 1994. Reprinted by permission of *Ms.* Magazine, ©1994.

it; because on TV violence is both glorified and simplified; and because it even gives people ideas).

When I have tried to engage them in dialogue over the issue, I find my children's sophistry daunting: *Teenage Mutant Ninja Turtles* is not violent, they claim, because it is a cartoon, and cartoons are funny; *MacGyver* is not harmful, because the hero doesn't carry a gun; and, besides, they argue, both of the above are hard to distinguish from the news shows grownups

> *"Statistics . . . put cartoons at the top of the list of violent fare."*

watch. They would not be impressed, although I am, by statistics assembled in a 1992 *TV Guide* study that put cartoons at the top of the list of violent fare, followed by toy commercials(!). And although MacGyver may be unarmed, the promotions for his show were cited as having among the highest number of incidents of gunplay and physical assault; the newscasts aired only a tame fraction of the same.

The Connection between Television and Violence

The National Center for Juvenile Justice estimates that there were 247,000 violent crimes committed by minors in 1992 (the most recent year for which data are available). We know that before they are out of grade school, most of our children have seen some 8,000 murders and 100,000 acts of violence on television. Any parent can tell you that there is a connection between these numbers, regardless of the ongoing debate among experts. In a poll of 71,000 *USA Weekend* readers, 86 percent said that they "notice changes in [their] kids' behavior after they've seen a violent show." While some parents I know witness increased aggressiveness, there are other responses; I have found that sometimes my kids become more passive, detached, "spaced out." It seems that boys are more drawn to the shows and more agitated by them; girls, for the most part, are repelled, even saddened by them.

Whether these differences in children's responses are a function of nature or environment is a perplexing issue for parents, one that highlights the gray area between cause and effect—and therefore complicates the debate over suggested remedies. For example, a bill proposed by Senators Daniel Inouye (D.-Hawaii) and Ernest Hollings (D.-S.C.) to limit the kinds of shows broadcast during peak viewing hours for children raises important questions about freedom and responsibility. Proponents of the bill point to studies that show children exposed to a heavy diet of blood and guns become desensitized to real violence and, at the same time, excessively fearful of becoming victims. But the very persuasive arguments against such legislation center around the risks of censorship. Television's First Amendment protection *is* limited by a federal statute that instructs the Federal Communications Commission to make sure that TV stations operate in the "public interest." But any further effort to restrict content opens a

Pandora's box. Whenever I say to myself, "Children shouldn't be allowed to see this stuff!" I am reminded that the same motives were behind efforts I deplored to remove from library shelves such "offensive material" as *The Diary of Anne Frank*, *The Adventures of Tom Sawyer*, and *Our Bodies, Ourselves*.

Necessary Violence

Efforts to explain the relationship between violence imagined and violence committed lead into other mazes. World-renowned child psychologist Bruno Bettelheim made the disturbing observation that the ghoulish fairy tales that show up in every culture are necessary vehicles for children to work out their violent impulses and to come to terms with their own hearts of darkness.

My own childhood experience with grim fairy tales (Hans Christian Andersen, in my case) has made me leery of parental prudishness. I remember my mother reading me a story called "The Girl Who Trod on a Loaf." It went something like this: "There was a very vain girl who loved her beautiful clothes. One muddy day she went out to buy bread, and on the way home, she came across a big puddle. She didn't want to get her party shoes dirty so she put the loaf down and stepped on it instead . . ." And? And nothing. I must have seen that there were more pages to the story, or perhaps I sensed my mother's internal censor cutting the narrative off, because soon after I was able to read, I went back to that story and found that indeed it goes on into a horrendous climax in which the girl is sucked through the mud puddle into a subterranean hell where she is punished for her vanity. To this day it is the only fairy tale I remember, and the horror of the story is compounded by the distress I felt at uncovering my mother's subterfuge.

The Television Violence Reduction Through Parental Empowerment Act—better known as the V-Chip Bill—proposed by Edward Markey (D.-Mass.) would do just what my mother tried to do: banish the bad stuff. There is something too neat and clean about putting a microchip in the TV that would alert parents to violent programming and allow them to block it out. It has obvious immediate appeal, but does it give parents the false confidence that by pushing a button, they have fulfilled their responsibility to articulate and "sell" their values to their children? And how would you protect your children from the promos for the off-limits violent movies and series that, according to the *TV Guide* study, "have become a major source of televised violence"? On a strictly pragmatic level, I know that the Girl-Who-Trod-on-a-Loaf principle will ensure that my children will ultimately see the proscribed show—most likely at a friend's house—at which time they will probably pay closer attention than usual because of the taboo at home.

> *"The ghoulish fairy tales that show up in every culture are necessary vehicles for children to work out their violent impulses."*

The instructive power of violent images is evoked by Walter Wink, a professor of biblical interpretation at Auburn Theological Seminary in New York City. In his book *Engaging the Powers*, Wink writes that "violence is so successful as a myth precisely because it does not appear to be mythic in the least. Violence simply appears to be the nature of things." Children's entertainment says Wink reflects the "myth of redemptive violence" as played out in the classic plot line:

> Children identify with the good guys so that they can think of themselves as good. This enables them to project out onto the bad guy their own repressed anger, violence, rebelliousness, or lust and then vicariously to enjoy their own evil by watching the bad guy initially prevail. . . . When the good guy finally wins, viewers are then able to reassert control over their own inner tendencies, repress them, and reestablish a sense of goodness. Salvation is guaranteed through identification with the hero.

The redemptive value of this morality play is challenged by such real-life findings as those of Leonard Eron, a professor of psychology at the University of Michigan who monitored a group of kids for over 20 years. He concluded that the more frequently they watched violent television at age 8, the more serious were the crimes they were convicted of by 30, the more aggressive their behavior when drinking, and the harsher the punishment they inflicted on their own children.

"The more frequently [children] watched violent television at age 8, the more serious were the crimes they were convicted of by 30."

The crusading founder of Action for Children's Television, Peggy Charren, responds to such studies with characteristic directness: "Poverty is what you fix if you want to do something about violence." She spoke at a *TV Guide* symposium on television violence and children, where she described the work she has done to bring about changes in children's programming; although her group no longer exists, its mission has been picked up by the Washington, D.C.–based Center for Media Education. Meanwhile, public anxiety is rising to a desperate level. A Times Mirror Center for the People & the Press study has found that 80 percent of those interviewed felt violence on TV was "harmful to society." I am among that 80 percent. What can we do?

What the Public Can Do

First of all, we can protest—to the stations, the producers, the advertisers. (We should also praise, with equal vigor, shows that please us.) We can urge them to adopt a rating system that will alert parents to particularly lethal shows—ABC announced an 800-number to call for parental advisories on specific programming. We can try harder to monitor the programs that our kids watch. And we can try to put simulated violence into a larger moral context.

A recurrent worry expressed at the congressional hearings was that young viewers are seeing a sanitized kind of punching, stabbing. and killing. How to reconnect violence with pain and suffering in their minds? "Make it grisly," advises TV critic Marvin Kitman. When Gloucester is blinded in the 1983 Granada TV production of *King Lear*, Kitman reminds us, we are forced to focus on "those bloody rags" he uses to cover the ravaged eye sockets, which "said something special about the enormity of the vio-

> *"We can try harder to monitor the programs that our kids watch."*

lence wrought." Kitman may have identified a positive use for the "if it bleeds, it leads" format embraced by most local TV news programs: a reality fix on violence. When we invite our children to join us watching the news (after stressing to them that the world is not a uniformly violent place, that good and peaceful deeds are taking place all the time, only not on camera) we might be able to use the litany of crime and cruelty as "bloody rags"—reminders that when violence strikes, real people bleed and suffer and die, and real people mourn them. One local television station—WCCO in Minneapolis—is trying out a "family sensitive" five o'clock news broadcast that reports crime but saves the pictures for eleven. This format has possibilities, but it remains to be seen whether newswriters will take the opportunity to create an instructive context that could help families deal with the crime stories.

In the opposite vein, we can find ways to heighten a child's awareness of the artifice that makes a pretend punch look real and a real actor appear to be blown apart by a submachine gun. I would welcome a violence counterpart to a very effective aid I have found for explaining advertising to my kids. I taped an HBO special called *Buy Me That* that demystifies the techniques used by makers of commercials for children's toys. One segment begins by showing an ad in which several kids are hopping happily on a sort of pogo stick, as if it were the easiest thing in the world; then the toy is given to a group of real kids who try to hop. They fall off; they hurt themselves; many give up. In another segment, the maker of cereal commercials explains that glue is poured onto cereal (yuk!) because it looks whiter than milk. My kids watch the show over and over and are experts at detecting similar gimmicks in TV commercials. The spell has clearly been broken.

Remedial Programming

It would certainly be possible to do the same with scenes of violence: to explain exactly how blood shows up on the clean white shirt of a victim or how the noise of a punch is made or how a retractable knife blade simulates a stabbing; and it would be great to interview a stunt man or woman about the athletic expertise it takes to jump from a building or simply to fall down dead.

Another kind of remedial programming would dramatize convincing alternatives to a body blow. We know that, in the same way that violent families produce violent children, a limited vocabulary of alternatives for conflict resolution produces a reflexive use of violence. Elizabeth Thoman, executive director of the Center for Media Literacy in Los Angeles, advises parents to explore with their children alternatives to stories that focus on violence as the solution to interpersonal conflict. In the same vein, Kitman proposes a policy modeled on the fairness doctrine, which used to require giving equal airtime to conflicting political points of view. It would mandate a balance of programs that deal with conflict and anger in ways that are nonviolent.

Kitman's suggestion recalls the truism that television's weakness is also its strength: it is one of the most effective teaching tools we have. Dr. Deborah Prothrow-Stith of the Harvard School of Public Health is thinking of ways to use the best of the medium to combat the worst. She suggests the campaign against smoking as an analogy. "We went from thinking it was the most glamorous thing in the world to finding it offensive and unhealthy," she points out at the *TV Guide* symposium. "How did we do that? It was education in the classroom. It was working with the media. We banned the advertising of cigarettes on television." She thinks we can perform a similar change of attitudes about violence. So does Charren, who has an imaginative suggestion of her own, a "media-literacy merit badge" for Girl and Boy Scouts. "It's a way to teach kids that the violence you see on television is not the solution to problems," she says.

> *"We can find ways to heighten a child's awareness of the artifice that makes a pretend punch look real."*

While such ideas are building toward a nationwide campaign to heal the bruised hearts and minds of our children, I take my hat off to one innovative father I have heard about. He would let his child watch *Teenage Mutant Ninja Turtles* cartoons, but only if the child would imagine a fifth turtle named Gandhi. Later they would discuss how "Ninja Gandhi" might get the turtles out of trouble without violence. I am equally impressed by the legendary parent who lures her kids away from the evil box with an invitation to an impromptu spring picnic. But my true (and secret) role model is the one who can effectively command "Turn the TV off—*now* . . . because I say so!" I am none of the above. But I'm trying. And I believe that as long as we keep struggling with the system and with our children, we are teaching at the only level that really counts—by what we do, not what we say.

Chapter 5

Does Music
Promote Violence?

CURRENT CONTROVERSIES

Chapter Preface

In the late 1950s Elvis Presley introduced a new kind of music to many Americans. His rock-and-roll rhythms and gyrating style fascinated many teenagers and worried many parents. When the singer appeared on Ed Sullivan's variety show, Presley's hips were kept out of the range of the camera because his movements were considered too suggestive.

Looking back on the Presley-Sullivan incident, many people are amused at the innocence of the time and the situation. Today people are still concerned about how music might affect the young and society as a whole. But the primary worry today is the violent content of some songs, such as the lyrics of "Cop Killer," a 1992 song by the rapper Ice-T:

> I'm 'bout to bust some shots off
> I'm 'bout to dust some cops off . . .
> Die, Die, Die Pig, Die!

These lyrics angered police, politicians, and the public, who all feared that the song would incite people to kill police. But Ice-T defended the song and his intent: "It's only aimed at those cops who think the badge allows them to mistreat people. If a cop treats me like a regular human being, I got all the respect for him."

Others who also defend violent lyrics in rap and rock music add that such lyrics serve a purpose. Michael Small, author of a book on rap music, *Break It Down*, argues that "despite highly reported incidents of crimes committed by fans and a few rappers, the link between rap and violence is not clear. . . . Today's roughest rhymes sometimes help to relieve tension. Rap gives kids some control over the haphazard violence that surrounds them, translating it into pugnacious—but basically safe—music."

Critics, however, point to cases such as that of Ronald Ray Howard, a nineteen-year-old who killed a Texas state trooper in 1992. Howard contended that he was inspired by the antipolice lyrics in the music of rapper Tupac Shakur (who himself was sentenced in 1995 to a six-year jail term for assaulting a female fan). This case and others lead some to agree with writer Nathan McCall: "There are obviously some correlations between the constant, negative, violent messages that are being put out in rap and the violence that exists out there in the real world."

Many rap and rock songs have violent lyrics. But whether these lyrics are powerful enough to incite real-life violence, and whether they should be censored or regulated, is controversial. The following chapter presents arguments that support and oppose violent lyrics in music and the right of musicians to perform such music.

Heavy Metal Rock and Gangsta Rap Music Promote Violence

by Barbara Hattemer and Robert Showers

About the authors: *Barbara Hattemer is the president of the National Family Foundation, an organization that studies families and promotes ways to strengthen them. Robert Showers is an attorney. They are the authors of the book* Don't Touch That Dial, *from which this viewpoint is excerpted.*

> Dances suggesting or representing sexual actions or indecent passion are forbidden. Dances which emphasize indecent movements are to be regarded as obscene.
>
> —The Motion Picture Code, 1930–1966

"Music and singing have played an important role in the learning and memorization process for centuries," [states Bob DeMoss in the video "Rising to the Challenge"]. The success of *Sesame Street* in combining music, words, and colorful images to make learning fun and easy illustrates that children do learn what they see role modeled before them, especially when it is set to music.

Destructive Influence

Grade school children and adolescents today are exposed to role models vastly different from those offered by *Sesame Street*. The music, words, and colorful images of rock music videos are influencing increasingly younger children in progressively destructive directions.

"The rock video is generating the beat for today's youth," [Barry L. Sherman and Laurence W. Etling state. They also argue that] the rise of the youth culture over the past thirty years "has been one of the most dramatic aspects of a cultural change in American society since the adoption of motorized travel," and the music video as displayed on cable channel MTV has been extremely influential in shaping that culture. As radio was the "tribal drum" that sent the message to America's youth in the early days of rock music, the music videos of MTV proclaim the message to today's youth culture.

Music television burst into our living rooms in August 1981. Now "free" on most basic cable stations, it has over fifty-four million family subscribers. A whole generation has been molded and influenced by it. Indeed, it has sparked fashion trends, saved the record industry from decline, and introduced the nation's children to a new vocabulary of profanity, sex, and violence.

> *"Music television . . . [has] introduced the nation's children to a new vocabulary of profanity, sex, and violence."*

MTV is the cable channel most watched by college students. Informal surveys show that it is also becoming the favorite of nine- to eleven-year-olds in grade school. It is particularly intriguing for pre-teens who aspire to leave childhood behind and become "teen-agers." Nothing introduces them to the worst elements of the "grown-up" world faster than heavy metal rock music.

When not listening to MTV, children listen to rock music on radio. Both children and teens spend an average of a little over three hours a day watching television, but they spend four to six hours a day listening to music. That is eleven thousand hours between the seventh and twelfth grades. High volume and the use of headphones eliminate competing noises, enhancing the "impact of the music and its message," according to Joseph Stuessy. Unlike parents, rock music stars are always available to offer unqualified acceptance to young people hungry for attention and understanding. They appear to meet their needs and understand their chaotic emotions better than their own parents. Research has found that listening to heavy metal music correlates with increasing discomfort in family situations, a preference for friends over family, and poor academic performance. Rock music has become one of the primary means of group identification with individuals in the youth culture. "For many, the bonding agent of their friendship is music, mainly heavy metal," as Stuessy concludes.

Although the effects of the lyrics are virtually untested, teenagers have more sustained contact with heavy metal music than they have with either pornography or horror films. This type of music has been accused not only of being indecent, but obscene, violent, and satanic. Dr. Paul King found it to be correlated with increased chemical dependence, violence, stealing, and sexual activity. Reflecting hedonism (pleasure-seeking) and irresponsibility, rock music is symbolic of the clash of values between parents and their children. Described as "primitive" and inciting "baser passions," it reflects youth "at odds with adult society," [according to Larson and Robert Kubey].

The Harms of Rock

In 1989, the American Medical Association released a report that concluded that music is a greater influence in the life of a teen-ager than television. Those involved in the rock culture were more likely to be low achievers, involved in drugs, sexually active, and involved in satanic activities. Saying that the issue is too complicated to prove a one-on-one correlation, they nonetheless concluded that a fascination with heavy metal music was an indicator of adolescent alienation and possible emotional health problems. One study [by the American Medical Society] found that "seventh and tenth graders who watched an hour of rock videos were more likely to approve of premarital sex" than those who did not watch. Because much of the material is too pornographic and violent to deliberately show children, such studies are scarce. If, however, one hour of milder material influences attitudes, certainly four hours every day of heavy metal rock produces even more dramatic results.

> *"Heavy metal and rap music today contains an element of hatred and abuse of women of a degree never seen before."*

"Music has the power to form character," Aristotle said. According to Bob DeMoss, an expert on the popular culture who has studied the effect of rock music lyrics and images on children for many years, the early themes of rock music were "Drug abuse is okay," "Casual sex is fine," and "Violence is an acceptable form of behavior." Since the mid-1980s, these themes have degenerated to such explicit and graphic images and words, they almost defy description.

Extraordinary Sexism and Racism

The names of heavy metal bands reflect their character, image, and message. Free Congress' report on rock music lists 238 of them.

> . . . There are at least 13 bands named after the male genitals, 6 after female genitals, 4 after sperm, 8 after abortion and one after a vaginal infection. . . . [There are also] at least 10 bands named after various sex acts, 8 including the F-word, and 24 referring unflatteringly to blacks, the disabled or homosexuals.

The report comments that "heavy metal and rap music today contains an element of hatred and abuse of women of a degree never seen before." In addition to extraordinary sexism, they contain equally offensive racism, blasphemy, and bigotry. Regarding CBS Records president Walter Yetnikoff's comment "when the issue is bigotry, there is a fine line of acceptable standards which no piece of music should cross": This principle of acceptable standards applies to much more than bigotry.

In December 1984, *Life* magazine labeled heavy metal rock music a "sado-masochistic nightmare." The themes conveyed by images of wild expressions, painted faces, blood pouring from mouths, blood spurting from bodies, guns, knives, leather, chains, spikes, and ropes fall roughly into five overlapping categories:

1. *Aggressive Rebellion.*

You don't need those people around and that includes your parents. (Gene

Simmons from Kiss)

Rock stars openly encourage children to rebel against their parents; not the normal rebellion that helps a child separate from his parents emotionally, but a vicious and angry rebellion, full of hatred and violence.

In the video "We're Not Gonna Take It" by Twisted Sister, a father becomes angry at his young son for listening to rock music, and the boy hurls him through a plate glass window. This video inspired a young man in New Mexico to murder his father in similar fashion.

Dr. King wrote that "marketing heavy metal musicians as glamour figures and their message of hate as mere rebellion is confusing to youngsters who are trying to decide who they should be and what kind of behavior is appropriate for them."

2. *Abuse of Drugs and Alcohol.*

> We've always been serious alcoholics . . . no kidding around. (Nicky Sixx of Motley Crue)

> I took LSD every day for years. I went through cocaine by the bagful. . . . I O.D.'d about a dozen times, I sampled heroin, too. (Ozzy Osbourne)

Heavy metal music affirms anti-social, drug-addictive behavior. Not surprisingly, nearly 60 percent of chemically dependent youngsters chose heavy metal music because they considered it the musical expression of forces at work in their lives—violence, promiscuous sex, drug use, and increasingly, satanism.

Music for Insecure Teens

Dr. King compared music preferences with participation in violent behavior for 470 adolescent patients over three years. Heavy metal music was the choice of 59 percent admitted for chemical dependency. Of those, 74 percent were involved in violence, 50 percent in stealing, and 71 percent in sexual activity.

> *"Rock stars openly encourage children to rebel against their parents."*

Large numbers of disturbed adolescents with low self-worth draw inspiration from heavy metal because it makes them feel powerful and in charge. Providing simple answers to complex problems, it gives them a source of authority for what they feel and do.

3. *Graphic Violence and Suicide.*

> The blade of my knife, faced away from your heart
> Those last few nights, it turned and sliced you apart
> Laid out cold, now we're both alone
> But killing you helped me keep you home.
> ("Girls, Girls, Girls," Motley Crue)

> In goes my knife, pull out his life,
> Consider that bastard dead.
> ("Shout at the Devil," Motley Crue)

No apparent motive, just kill and kill again,
Survive my brutal slashing, I'll hunt you till the end.
("Hell Awaits," Slayer)

A baseball cap with the letters AC-DC embroidered on it and a knapsack of heavy metal video tapes were found at one of the murder sites of the Los Angeles Night Stalker, who killed sixteen victims by slipping into their homes at night and shooting or stabbing them to death as they slept.

I'm your night prowler, I sleep in the day
Yes, I'm your night prowler, get out of my way.
("Night Prowler" from AC-DC's *Highway to Hell*)

In a study of twelve hundred rock videos, the National Coalition on Television Violence found 45 percent of them violent in nature. Researcher Hannelore Wass speculated that rock music should be understood as a metaphor, that "killing someone or practicing satanism might stand for power, while . . . self-destruction

> *"Our culture has not yet discovered how to deal with entertainment that spews forth sheer hatred."*

might stand for depression and a sense of isolation." Meanwhile, according to Phyllis Schlafly, more than "5,000 teenagers are committing suicide each year, double the rate of 25 years ago." The mounting statistics on teen suicide are more than symbolic. They indicate young people take these messages literally.

Suicide Notes

Two fifteen-year-old girls left suicide notes that quoted lyrics from Pink Floyd's 1979 album, *The Wall*. They wrote, "Goodbye cruel world, I'm leaving you now."

John McCullum's parents brought a suit against Ozzy Osbourne after their son committed suicide while listening to his song:

Where to hide, suicide is the only way out
Don't you know what it's really about.
("Suicide Solution," Ozzy Osbourne)

4. *Fascination with the Occult.*

I am possessed by all that is evil, the death of your God I demand, I spit at the virgin you worship, and sit at Lord Satan's right hand. . . .
("Welcome to Hell," Venom)

We are instruments of evil, we come straight out of hell.
We're the legions of the demons, haunting for the kill.
("Demons," Rigor Mortis)

In North Port, New York, a devil-worshipping cult called The Knights of the Black Circle gathered at a park and performed rituals that killed Gary Lauwers, 17, stabbing him while forcing him to say "I love Satan," and later gouging out his eyes. They left the names of their favorite rock stars: Black Sabbath and Ozzy Osbourne, who sings of satanic possession and once bit off a dove's head during a performance.

The following description of satanic involvement in rock videos was taken from the Congressional Record:

> The satanic message is clear, both in the album covers and in the lyrics, which are reaching impressionable young minds. . . . The symbolism is all there: the satanic pentagram, the upside-down cross, the blank eyes of the beast, the rebellion against Christianity, and again and again, the obsession with death. According to most groups, it's all done in fun. But according to police it's having an effect on many children, a growing subculture that mixes heavy metal music with drugs and the occult.
>
> *The police chief estimated that heavy metal music indicators were found at 35 to 40 percent of the investigations of crimes involving satanic worship.* (emphasis added) . . .

5. *Sexuality That Is Graphic and Explicit* .

> I f——k like a beast.
> ("The Torture Never Ends," W.A.S.P.)

> I know a girl named Nikki. I guess you could say she was a sex fiend, I met her in a hotel lobby masturbating with a magazine.
> ("Darling Nikki," Prince from *Purple Rain*)

While rock music has always been associated with sex, it has gone so far beyond innuendo there is nowhere left to go in graphic explicitness:

(1) *Incest:* "Incest is everything it's said to be"—from the song "Sister" by Prince.

(2) *Oral sex:* "Eat Me Alive" by Judas Priest is about forced oral sex at gun point.

(3) *Cross dressing/transvestite:* Alice Cooper "rose to fame by giving his fans exhibitions of transvestitism, snakes, mutilating chickens and mock executions [as noted in the *Miami Herald*]."

(4) *Bondage and torture:*

> Tie her down, she knows what's waiting for her.
> Nothing too cruel, so beat her 'til she's red and raw,
> Crack the whip, it hardly stings the bitch.
> ("She Likes It Rough," Thrasher)

> Forbidden techniques, it's just what they seek
> Fantasy lane, dominance, submission, handcuffs and chains,
> Bondage and pain . . .
> ("Dungeons of Pleasure," Nasty Savage)

There is hard-core pornography on record albums, posters, fan magazines, and concert stages. DeMoss says, "It is hard to distinguish between the two [regular and music-related pornography] except the latter is legally available to children." The erotic costumes of hard-core pornography magazines like *Bizarre Bitches* have been copied by bands like Bitch in concert and pictured in teen fan magazines.

Perhaps the most brutal is W.A.S.P.'s lead singer, Blackie Lawless, who has appeared on stage wearing a buzz-saw blade between his thighs. During "The Torture Never Stops," he pretends to beat a woman wearing only a G-string and a black hood. As blood pours out from her hood, he attacks her with the blade.

Sut Jhally, an associate professor of communications at the University of Massachusetts, put together 165 scenes from rock videos to make *Dreamworlds: Desire/Sex/Power in Rock Video.* It reveals the direct relationship between the presentation of women for male consumption in these videos and "the prevalence of date rape and sexual violence in this country." Juxtaposing a real rape scene between actual videos, he demonstrates the end result of presenting women as nymphomaniacs in a male adolescent dream world.

Every parent and public policy maker should see one of the many good videos that have been produced to show how extreme the performances of heavy metal bands have become. No amount of research or written description can have the cumulative impact of actually seeing it.

The Hate Messages in Rap

Hearing the hate messages of today's rap music can be equally unsettling. Just as the police are taking satanic rock music seriously, they are suddenly taking rap's messages of killing policemen seriously. According to *Newsweek*, "Police organizations around the country called for a boycott of Time Warner over a song called 'Cop Killer,' by the Warner Records rapper Ice-T." Lyrics include

I'm bout to bust some shots off
I'm bout to dust some cops off
. . . Die, Die, Die Pig, Die.

As South Florida's Sheriff Don Hunter tried to tell a deaf local media, "Murder is not art."

Newsweek speaks of rap's "ability to alienate," of "its imagery, sound and lyrics" being "pure confrontation." As rap music attempts to define black culture and racism, it educates us all on the "hell" of inner-city life—"its gangs, lack of self-esteem, crime, rage, murder"—and fills the heads of tuned-in children with rebellion, hate, and more raw sex. Like sex, "violence sells." Kids tune in because they like "that violent thing."

> *"The lyrics . . . were described as 'alienated, negativistic, nihilistic, and pornographic.'"*

Like rebellious heavy metal, rap has found its home on MTV. In it, MTV has found "a music equal to its visual jump-cutting rhythms." But our culture has not yet discovered how to deal with entertainment that spews forth sheer hatred. As the Supreme Court rules in favor of hateful speech, young blacks from the ghetto are free to advocate hate and murder to all troubled youths, who seem eager to absorb it. . . .

The rock video is little more than a marketing tool to reach the youth market, roughly from twelve to thirty-four years of age. Profit-oriented, it deliberately "creates an unreal environment" to motivate people to buy recordings, [states Levy]. Offbeat themes and startling images result from the struggle to attract and maintain viewers' attention. The easiest way to accomplish that is excessive amounts of sex and violence.

> *"Hatred, violence, and perversion are not less influential because they are set to music. They are in fact more powerful."*

I'll either break her face or I'll take down her legs, get my ways at will.
("Too Fast for Love," Motley Crue)

. . . heart ripped from the chest decapitated, a meal of vaginas and breasts.
("Predator," Genocide)

A 1986 content analysis of forty hours of music videos on three networks found that "music videos are violent, male-oriented and laden with sexual content." Sex was linked to violence in 80 percent of the videos containing violence. A 1983 study revealed that in more than half of the videos females were either nude or wore highly seductive clothing or undergarments.

Drs. C.H. Hansan and R.D. Hansan report music videos to be high in sex and violence and portraying "rebellion against parental and lawful authority, drunkenness, promiscuity, and derogation and devaluation of women, the work ethic and family values," presenting anti-social behavior in a favorable light and as desirable and commonplace. . . .

A causal link between viewing music videos and negative behaviors has not been established in the research literature. However, it is highly likely that their role as a socializing agent is more important than any measurable short term changes. [Gerbner, Gross and Morgan, and other] researchers have already found that television "plays a disproportionate role in the cultivation of social concepts," communicating values, relationships, and beliefs about life and society. Since MTV is the favorite channel of multitudes of children, it is clear that rock videos play a large part in the socialization process. . . .

They Know and Like the Words

In 1986, the University of Florida (Gainesville) surveyed the rock music preferences of 694 middle and high-school students. The survey found that 9 percent of middle school students, 17 percent of rural, and 24 percent of urban high-school students were fans of heavy metal rock and punk rock music, which promotes homicide, satanism, and suicide. The lyrics in the study defied "any reasonable adult standard concerning the value of human life and Judeo-Christian and humanistic beliefs," [states Hannelore Wass]. They were described as "alienated, negativistic, nihilistic, and pornographic . . . promoting sex, sado-masochism, rape, killing, satanic practices, and in some instances suicide."

Heavy metal fans listened to rock music more than thirty hours per week, and they reported knowing the lyrics of "all" their favorite rock songs more than did fans of general rock music. Almost twice as many heavy metal fans as general rock fans felt that it was proper for young children to listen to destructive rock music and that they would not in any way be affected. That most adolescents know many or all of the lyrics has been reported by others as well. In this case, many heavy metal fans reported agreeing with the words. Adolescents in this study who were not heavy metal fans reported concern for the effects of the music on children, often as a result of seeing their own friends affected.

A follow-up study looked at the music preferences of 120 adolescent offenders in two youth detention centers. They found that 54 percent of them were heavy metal fans, compared to less than 20 percent in the earlier study. Among the delinquent youths, the number was three times as high. "This finding suggests a strong relationship between antisocial or destructive behavior and preference for rock music with destructive themes." Dr. Wass recommended that mental health professionals "consider adolescents' music-related behaviors and orientations as a useful indicator for psychological assessment.". . .

Dr. King's research has shown that "at the very least, heavy metal music promotes, approves, and supports unconventional attitudes toward drug abuse, sexual activity and violence." Whether or not it directly causes aberrant behavior, he believes it constitutes a public health problem "serious enough to warrant some type of control." He recommends that major record companies, with the help of physicians, set forth guidelines "to ensure that potentially harmful material is not sold to our young people packaged as entertainment."

As both research and anecdotal evidence mounts to prove Dr. King's assertion, responsible music companies must adopt more responsible policies. If they do not, government regulation is inevitable. There is a groundswell of fear among adults that the subculture is already out of control and that soon we will all be threatened. Hatred, violence, and perversion are not less influential because they are set to music. They are in fact more powerful.

The industry has resisted even the labeling of X-rated records. Chances of rock stars taking responsibility without parental and governmental pressure are next to nothing. Therefore, parents must encourage the Federal Communications Commission to be more diligent in efforts to enforce the decency standard on broadcast radio and television and help them by sending in cases. Since MTV has become readily available to children on basic cable, this standard should be extended to cable in the form of a "harmful to minors" law. Removing MTV from basic cable and making it a separate subscription channel that parents could realistically keep from their homes is an even better solution.

Gangsta Rap Promotes Violence in the Black Community

by Nathan McCall

About the author: *Nathan McCall graduated from Norfolk State University in Virginia after spending three years in prison for armed robbery. He is a reporter for the* Washington Post *and the author of the book* Makes Me Wanna Holler: A Young Black Man in America.

Gangsters, guns and violence have always held a fascination for Americans, and blacks like me are no different. I'll never forget the first time I went with some buddies in the early 1970s to see *The Godfather*. I was mesmerized by the movie's shootouts, retaliatory murders and the ruthless gangster code. They had a way of resolving conflict that was appealing to a teen-ager trying to work through the murky rites of manhood. The message I picked up was: if somebody double-crosses you, he deserves to die. *The Godfather* was fantasy, but to a bunch of spirited boys it was a celebration of machismo.

I eventually got my chance to do the Godfather thing when an older guy in the neighborhood threatened my girl. Because that dude had offended my lady and, by extension, disrespected me, I concluded: he deserves to die.

Mixed Up in the Head

I was 19, and it didn't take much to push me into reckless action. When I ran into that man, I gunned him down. It was like one great fantasy, as glorious as the gangland slayings in the movie. After he collapsed, I stood over him, proud that I'd upheld the Godfather code. But later that night, as I was fingerprinted and booked in a police station, the fantasy faded. That's when I shed my pseudo-gangster persona and discovered what I really was: a silly, scared teen-ager who was mixed up in the head.

When a policeman told my stepfather and me that the man I shot might die, I became mired in the weirdest illogic: if he died, I'd be charged with murder, yet I would have denied to the end that I was a murderer.

Why wasn't I prepared to accept the consequences of my actions? Because, on some level, I was certain that the person who shot that guy was not really me—it was some person I'd thought I wanted to be. I'd been fantasizing, and fantasies don't deal with consequences.

Lucky for me, he lived and I got off with a light sentence.

But I never stopped thinking about the shooting and the influences that had led me to do such things. I thought about it again recently while following reports of reformers trying to restrict TV and movie violence. Their efforts are a reminder of a child-rearing truism: young people bombarded with images of sex and violence often find it hard to separate fantasy from fact. And some can't resist the temptation to act out what they've seen.

> *"Young people bombarded with images of sex and violence often find it hard to separate fantasy from fact."*

If the reformers succeed, it will ensure that many kids get less exposure to graphic images, but any controls may overlook an area that's important to blacks. It seems to me that white kids are more plugged in to TV, and black kids are more into music, especially rap.

Not all rap is bad; in fact, much of it is brilliant. But more and more, the good stuff is being overshadowed by a torrent of obscene lyrics and graphic videos.

Especially troubling are the lyrics in "gangsta rap," which has become the dominant strain of the 1990s. It often denigrates women and glorifies guns and gangs. Consider this piece of advice from popular rapper Dr. Dre and imagine how it sounds to a young boy's ears:

> Rat-tat-tat-tat-tat-tat-tat like that
> Never hesitate to put a nigga on his back . . .

Plain and simple, that is a boastful call for black men to kill one another. Lyrics like these have become so pervasive that they're the accepted norm.

Influential Music

It may seem crazy to tie music to behavior. But the history of African-Americans shows that, from the days of slavery to the present, music has always been an agent of change. And rap is more than rhyming words. It's the central part of a powerful cultural movement—hip-hop—that influences the way young blacks walk, talk, dress and think.

The key element is aggression—in the rappers' body language, tone and witty rhymes—that often leaves listeners hyped, on edge, angry.

In gangsta rap, women are "bitches and hos," disposable playthings who exist merely for men's abusive delight; it's cool to use any means necessary to get the things you want; and most important, it's admirable to be cold-blooded and hard. Check out this rap by Snoop Doggy Dogg:

> See it's a West Coast thing where I'm from

And if you want some get some bad enough take some
But watch the gun by my side
Because it represents me and the mother [expletive] East Side
So bow down to the Bow Wow

Gangsta rappers often defend their themes by saying they reflect reality. But the brutality they toast has not always been part of our reality. This is a case of life imitating art in the worst way.

Apparently, many rappers believe their own hype, and some don't hesitate to act on what they sing about: Flavor Flav was indicted on two counts of weapon possession stemming from a dispute with another man; Snoop Doggy Dogg has been indicted in connection with a murder.

Obviously, gangsta rap does not inspire every young listener to pick up a gun, but what, I wonder, is the impact of all this on people already at risk?

"While the vast majority of kids are able to take negative rap and put it in perspective, some of our most vulnerable ones are influenced," says Melvin Williams of the District of Columbia Commission on Mental Health Services. "Those young people who have faulty parenting or no parenting at all are particularly vulnerable to influences such as rap."

Psychologist Na'im Akbar, a former president of the Association of Black Psychologists, acknowledges that the effect of negative messages on young people is not something that can be quantified. "You can't prove that it's causative," he explains, "but it certainly is correlational."

Rising Juvenile Crime Rates

Here are some of those correlations: Black-on-black violence has escalated sharply since the late 1980s, when the popularity of gangsta rap was on the rise. The number of juveniles arrested for murder increased by more than 50 percent from 1988 to 1992. Juvenile violent-crime arrests increased at almost the same rate.

The change in the values and behavior of young blacks in rural towns is another example. With the spread of hip-hop music and videos, we've begun hearing more about random violence in such places as Kansas and North Carolina.

While we've been seeking complex sociological explanations for the surge in violence afflicting young blacks, part of the answer may be right under our collective noses—and ears. Young blacks look to rappers—

"'Gangsta rap'. . . often denigrates women and glorifies guns and gangs."

many of whom are only kids themselves—as people they want to emulate. And because they feel powerless, these youths are consumed with the symbols of power—guns and gangstas.

They imagine themselves as Godfathers and, sadly, some actually get up the nerve to act out such roles. So they spray gunfire into crowded swimming pools, as happened in Washington, D.C., where they also gun folks down on a recreation field, with the stray bullets killing a four-year-old girl. Too often, reality doesn't kick in until the handcuffs are slapped on, just as it happened to me.

There are things we can do to stop the violence assaulting our eyes and ears. For starters, we can hit the recording companies, the ones that produce this garbage, where it hurts—in their pockets. Also, as police groups showed when they took on Time Warner over rapper Ice-T's song "Cop Killer," the power of embarrassment is immense.

Some black stations, including WBLS-FM in New York and KACE-FM in Los Angeles, recently banned airplay of recordings that glorify drugs, sex, violence and abuse of women. Other black stations should follow suit. We should also denounce misguided rappers who spread messages of hate.

Many of us have been reluctant to take part in anything that could be seen as censorship. But, as psychologist Akbar says, "Freedoms have come to be used as a justification of anarchy. Someone has got to monitor civilized life."

Monitoring, and ultimately reining in, gangsta rap is no panacea for the problems confronting black America. But if black America is not prepared to give our children something better than violence and abuse to fantasize about, who will?

Gangsta Rap Promotes Violence Against Women

by *Glamour*

About the author: Glamour *magazine is a monthly publication of fashion, beauty, and women's issues.*

If you haven't heard the lyrics blasting out of a car window or seen the songs dramatized in TV videos, you're one of the lucky few. Even as America finally begins to confront its violent alter ego—by passing gun-control laws, debating new crime bills, even threatening to regulate TV shows—a disturbing sound-track throbs steadily in the background, mocking those efforts.

The music—gangsta rap—celebrates a world in which women are either "bitches" or "whores," and where disaffected young men have .9-millimeter-handgun solutions to minor slights. Life is a round of jail, drugs, police, gangs, parties and sexual depravity. Death is a given; attitude is all. Consider "Bitches Ain't Shit," from the best-selling album *The Chronic*, by Dr. Dre. The chorus sums up the role of women in their universe: "Bitches ain't shit but ho's and tricks/Lick on these nuts and suck the dick."

Big Sales

If these sentiments are shocking, they're also quite profitable; starting with a consumer base of inner-city youth, gangsta rap has also reaped big sales from suburban white kids. But the gangstas are building no cross-cultural bridges. The music's bestial lyrics reinforce racist stereotypes that African Americans have struggled for so long to erase. When white teens jam to Ice Cube or Dr. Dre (who, like most of the top sellers, won a 1994 Grammy award), they may be en-joying a vicarious rush of defiance, but they're receiving the message that may-hem and hatred of women are somehow intrinsic to the black urban lifestyle.

Now, a handful of radio stations—mostly black-owned and black-operated—have had enough: They have refused to play any more music that encourages vi-olence, promotes misogyny or reduces women to sexual objects. Instead, they've

"Women and 'Gangsta' Rap," *Glamour*, June 1994. Reprinted by permission.

elected to play edited versions of such songs or to scratch them off their playlists.

"We decided that we could get the sound we were looking for without playing music that didn't reflect the values of the community," says Ann McCullom, general manager of KACE/KAEV-FM in Los Angeles. The station, which began its policy in the summer of 1993, was the first in the nation to announce publicly that it would remove violent and sexist music from its playlist. In December 1993, WBLS-FM, a popular station in New York City, followed suit. Pierre Sutton, chairman, says that the station "did not want to contribute to the negative influences on WBLS's young listeners."

> *"The music—gangsta rap— celebrates a world in which women are either 'bitches' or 'whores.'"*

Is there, as some believe, a connection between listening to violent music (or watching violent TV shows) and committing violent acts? Gangsta rappers like to say that they aren't *advocating* anything—they are simply chronicling the frightening world they see around them. Both sides have a point—but consider the fact that such prominent gangsta rappers as Snoop Doggy Dogg and Tupac Shakur have been indicted on charges of murder and sexual assault, respectively (both have pleaded not guilty and as of May 1994 no trial dates had been set). Speaking about violence in music, at the Grammy Awards show in March 1994, host Garry Shandling wisecracked, "We're starting a Guns-for-Grammys swap program."

Plain Old Pornography

Gangsta proponents claim that the outcry against this kind of rap comes chiefly from the conservative, predominantly white watchdog groups who always seem to be pointing the finger at some form of popular culture. But the radio stations have now been joined in their protest by various black community groups, women's organizations and even a female rapper.

"Gangsta rap is plain old pornography," says C. DeLores Tucker, head of the National Political Congress of Black Women. In December 1993, her group held a press conference in the Senate urging the music industry to stop releasing gangsta-rap records that demean women and promote crime. In February 1994, Operation PUSH called for a controversial 40-day "fast" during which its supporters would not buy or listen to explicit, hardcore gangsta rap. PUSH founder Jesse Jackson later defended rap's defiance of police brutality, but stood firm that "we cannot call ourselves 'bitches' and 'niggers.' We fought hard to get away from that." Queen Latifah, a popular female rapper, talks back to the gangstas in her song "U.N.I.T.Y.," in which she tells women, "You *ain't* a bitch or a ho." And Carol Moseley-Braun (D.-Ill.), the only black female senator, has held one hearing on the issue and has plans for others.

But these are only first steps. Simply blaming rap music for the complex grid of social and economic factors that engender these hateful attitudes is facile and leads nowhere. Before we can hope for change, we must ask more difficult questions. Why do so many young black men feel threatened by black women? Why, at a time when the black community acknowledges the urgent need for unity, do so many black consumers support an art form that endorses chaos and self-hatred? And given the success of this music with mainstream audiences, black and white, what is the place of violence and misogyny in our *national* state of mind?

Rappers whose lyrics dwell on hatred and disregard for human life aren't journalists in the trenches or ethnographers out in the field. They are opportunists with a gift for rhyme, and the damage they do—to women, who are portrayed as little more than sexual receptacles, and to young black men, for whom homicide is the number-one cause of death—is real and long-lasting. Radio stations have caught up with them. Legislators are catching up with them. The rest of us still have some work to do.

Rap Music Should Be Censored

by Jonathan Alter

About the author: *Jonathan Alter is a columnist for* Newsweek *magazine.*

Imagine that a big record-company executive discovered a new skinhead band called Aryan Nation and distributed 2 million copies of a song with the lyrics: *Rat-a-tat and a tat like that / Never hesitate to put a nigga on his back.* This frank call for whites to kill blacks might run into a few problems around Hollywood. It's not likely, for instance, that Bill Clinton's advisers would recommend that their man appear at a gala fund-raiser at the executive's house. If radio stations declined to air Aryan Nation's songs advocating lynching, no one would scream "censorship."

Those lyrics in fact come from a rap song by Dr. Dre, whose label is Death Row/Interscope, which is part owned by Time Warner. Interscope is headed by Ted Field, a movie-and-record mogul who hosted Bill Clinton's big Hollywood fund-raiser in 1992. "A lot of this [criticism of rap] is just plain old racism," Field told the *Los Angeles Times*. "You can tell the people who want to stop us from releasing controversial rap music one thing: Kiss my ass."

Since Hollywood already has enough people who spend their days eagerly taking Ted Field up on that offer, I thought I'd try a different tack. It is Field and other phony liberals of his ilk, wrapping themselves in constitutional pieties, who are applying the racial double standards and devaluing legitimate civil-liberties concerns. It is they, more than the rappers themselves, who are responsible for spreading irresponsibility. And it is those who oppose them—private citizens rebuking or boycotting sociopathic entertainment—who are engaged in free expression in its best, most democratic sense.

Judgment, Not Censorship

That word—censorship—has been thrown around much too casually in recent years. If a record-company executive or an art-gallery owner or a book publisher declines to disseminate something, that's not censorship, it's judgment. It might be cowardly judgment or responsible judgment, but it is what they are paid to do. Garry Trudeau makes this point whenever some wimpy newspaper decides not to run a controversial *Doonesbury* strip: his fans say he was censored; he rightly calls it bad editing.

How did we get to a point where "art" became a code word for money? As record executive David Geffen said about Time Warner chief Gerald Levin's lame rationalizations for Ice-T's "Cop Killer," "To say that this whole issue is not about profit is silly. It certainly is not about artistic freedom." In other words, the Consti-

> *"If a record company . . . declines to disseminate something, that's not censorship, it's judgment."*

tution guarantees all Americans the right to rap, but it says nothing about Dr. Dre's right to a record contract.

In fact, if censorship means companies like Sony and Time Warner and Capitol Records begin to think harder about the messages they're sending young African-Americans, then maybe we need more of it. If censorship means executives bear greater personal accountability for what their companies produce—if it means that when Ted Field walks into a Beverly Hills restaurant, the patrons turn around and say with disgust, "Hey, that's the guy who tells blacks to shoot each other"—then it could help.

But that's not what the word means. Real censorship is when the government—*the government*—bans books in school libraries, prosecutes artists and writers for their work, seizes pornography, exercises prior restraint. And there's the whiff of censorship when the government hints at future action, as Janet Reno did with the TV networks. The line here gets tricky. Tipper Gore was way ahead of her time, and she never advocated censorship, only voluntary labeling of albums. But as the wife of the vice president, she's probably wise to go light on the issue now. Otherwise it might begin to feel censorious. A few private institutions—like schools that try to punish offensive student speech—could also be categorized as engaging in real censorship.

Doing What Is Responsible

Beyond that, let's give the word a rest. I was once a judge for a journalism contest sponsored by a group called Project Censored. The goal was to identify underreported or ignored stories, not officially censored ones. Such casual use of the word demeans victims of real censorship, here and abroad. So does describing the battle over government funding of controversial art as a "censorship" issue. This is loopy. Declining to use taxpayer dollars to fund art is hardly the same as suppressing it. When Los Angeles radio station KACE-FM recently took the commendable step of banning "socially irresponsible" music from its format, this, too, was attacked by some other radio stations as censorship.

These other stations routinely fail to play any folk music. Are they censoring Peter, Paul and Mary? Of course not. They're simply making a business assessment that folk is a ratings loser. What's annoying is the implicit assumption that choosing songs on the basis of what sells is somehow superior to choosing them on the basis of what's responsible.

If an editor wants to change the text of an article about ghetto life, that's editing. But if a rap producer wants to change sociopathic lyrics, that's seen as censorship. Even if you assume that rap is superior esthetically to journalism, is it really more worthy of protection? Is rap an inherently more valid form of expression than prose with no beat behind it? After all, they are both "voices of the community," waiting to be heard. So is Aryan Nation.

This is not an argument for applying a harsh moral standard to art, for easy listening everywhere on the dial, for record-company executives to sponsor nothing that they don't personally embrace. But even at its grimmest, music is meant to enhance life. Like tobacco executives, artists and record moguls who market death bear at least some responsibility for the consequences of their work. Let's confront that—and stop crying wolf on censorship.

Rap Music Is Unfairly Blamed for Society's Violence

by Tricia Rose

About the author: *Tricia Rose is an assistant professor of history and Africana studies at New York University. She is the author of the book* Black Noise: Rap Music and Black Culture in Contemporary America.

In these times, when media-crafted frenzies are the bread and butter of television news, entertainment programming, and tabloid journalism, street crime has become the coal that fires the crisis boiler. The notion that violent crime has swung out of control in this country is less a matter of fact and more a matter of perception constructed by law-and-order budget managers and ratings-hungry media executives. In fact, according to the FBI's National Crime Survey, burglary, homicides, and other violent crimes have decreased steadily since the mid 1970s.

Sexy Copy

Crime and violence have become the central focus of popular attention not because more and more people are the victims of crime, but because more Americans vicariously experience more violence through repetition of tabloid, televised news, and other reality-based programming. Street crime is sexy copy because, more than other equally pressing and even more urgent crises in American urban communities, it can be fitted into presentational formats crucial for mass media news consumption.

First, street crime lends itself to personal portraits of loss and horror; second, unlike corporate or economic crimes against people, it has clearly identifiable victims *and* villains, even when no villain is caught; third, it takes just one or two gruesome acts to terrorize viewers; and fourth, most street crime is committed by the least powerful members of society, those most easily vilified.

Other violent criminals with greater economic resources are less vulnerable to categorical public censure. Since reporting these sorts of crime appears to be a matter of public service, it creates the illusion that the terms of the discussion automatically are in the best interests of the public.

The Image of Crime Versus the Reality

In this whirlwind of produced, heightened, and repeated anxieties, it is essential to take a step back and distinguish between criminal acts and the social language used to talk about crime and to define criminals. It is important not to lose sight of the fact that these are not one and the same. In other words, crimes taking place are not the same thing as the perception of these crimes nor are they equivalent to the process of counting, naming, categorizing, and labeling criminal activity and ultimately criminalizing populations. (Think for a moment about the media explosion of child abuse cases and its relationship to the history of child abuse.)

These distinctions are not merely a matter of semantics. Understanding them allows people to see how the way they talk about a problem determines the solutions they deem logical and necessary. In other words, the terms of the discussion on crime in the public arena are helping set the direction of public policy.

In a still profoundly segregated and racially hierarchical society, popular public images and descriptions of poor black and Latino communities as hotbeds of crime, drugs, and violent behavior appear to be "mere descriptions" of the people and environments where crime takes place. These stories and pictures are not simply descriptive, however. They describe *some* elements of life in poor communities with a particular set of assumptions and consistently leave out and obscure descriptions of other parts.

The stories that frame violent street crimes deliberately omit information that would draw attention away from the sense of crisis produced by the depiction of an overwhelmingly horrible incident. "What," the stories often cry out, "would make a young person do such a thing?" Answers that might focus on the larger social picture—not flawed causal responses like poverty causes crime or there are more criminals so we need more prisons, but relational answers such as street crime is linked closely with unemployment and poverty—are deemed "excuses" by the logic of the story that surrounds it, not explanations.

> *"Anyone who is black and/or has lived in a poor black community knows that cops often equate suspicious behavior and black male bodies."*

The pity is that more information is not set forth about the conditions that foster such behaviors—the active municipal and corporate decisions that have exacerbated poverty, homelessness, and community instability. Relevant discourse could discourage current widespread public feelings of helplessness, bridge communities that do not currently see the similarities between them, and begin to lay the groundwork for a real examination of the vast and interdependent social forces and structures that have produced and transformed the face of street crime and destabilized the most fragile communities.

Institutional Violence

For all the public hue and cry about some categories of crime, rarely are Americans exposed to an informed exploration of the relationship between some kinds of crime and the extraordinary institutional violence done to the nation's poorest children of color. These include massive unemployment for them, their parents, and relatives; constant police harassment and violence against their peers, coupled with limited police efficacy against and in some cases complicity with the drug trade; routine arrests for "suspicious" behavior (anyone who is black and/or has lived in a poor black community knows that cops often equate suspicious behavior and black male bodies); appalling housing or none at all; limited access to legal or political redress; and dehumanizing state aid bureaucracies (such as demanding that welfare parents continually scour the listings for affordable apartments in order to keep their monthly rent coupons when the lowest market rentals cost two and three times more than their coupons can cover). This is topped off by economic shifts that have transformed the already bleak labor landscape in black urban communities into tenuous, low-pay, and dead-end service jobs.

> *"The white American public ... has been inundated with images of young black men who appear fully invested in a life of violent crime."*

Imagine how differently the same acts of violent street crime would read if they were coupled with stories that labeled these government-orchestrated institutional actions and neglects as acts of violence. What if these social policies that support the interests of the wealthy at the cruel expense of everyone else—especially the poor—were labeled acts of social violence? How then would Americans respond to the crime crisis? What policies would these criminal activities encourage?

Even more provocatively, what if we took a look at all crime (*e.g.*, domestic violence, embezzlement, the savings and loan scandal, serial killers, real estate fraud, murder, arson, rape, etc.) and highlighted the most consistent common denominator—men—and decided that, to solve the problem, it was necessary somehow to change the behavior of men as a group regardless of race and class. How would this alter our understanding of the crime dilemma? Instead of exploring these relationships, we are treated to disproportionately high visibility of a relatively small number of violent offenders who are intended to inspire fear in us. Without any relationship between these aspects of so-called social order and behavior of society's least powerful, the "real" answer implied by the constructed irrationality of street crime or participation in the drug trade is already present in the story: These are not people; they are monsters.

The demonization of young black males in the popular media, by black and white leaders and among law enforcement officials, has been well-documented by a range of scholars and others. This portrayal of young black men as unhuman—or dangerously superhuman, like the police fantasies of Rodney King—is an important part of creating a moral justification for the perpetuation of brutal and dehumanizing state policies. The white American public, many of whom only tangentially know any young black men personally, has been inundated with images of young black men who appear fully invested in a life of violent crime, who have participated in drug-related gang shoot-outs and other acts of violence for "no apparent reason."

> *"Most attacks on rap music offer profoundly shallow readings of its use of violent and sexist imagery."*

This last representation is crucial to the fear that current crime reporting encourages and to the work of demonizing. Such people are violent for no apparent reason; *they* are not like *us*. Isn't it reasonable to treat an animal like an animal? What rights and social obligations are extended to monsters?

Demonization is hard work. Making monsters out of a multitude of young people who struggle to survive under immense pressures involves drawing attention away from the difficulties they face, minimizing the abuses they suffer, and making their cultural activity seem a product or example of their status as dangerous creatures. "Representing" young black inner city males and "their ways" without considering black cultural literacy (especially hip hop) or devoting sufficient attention to larger structural forces and historical contextualization paves the way for readings of rap as the black monster's music. Adolescent and vernacular cultures always have tested the boundaries of acceptable speech, frequently exploring taboo and transgressive subjects. This is true of 18th-century English and Irish folk practices, the blues of the early 20th century, and rap today.

Overlooking Aesthetic Complexity

Most attacks on rap music offer profoundly shallow readings of its use of violent and sexist imagery and rely on a handful of provocative and clearly troubling songs or lyrics. Rarely is the genre described in ways that encompass the range of passionate, horrifying, and powerful storytelling in rap and gangsta rap. Few critics in the popular realm—there are some exceptions such as Robin D.G. Kelley, Maxine Waters (D.-Calif.), George Lipsitz, and Michael Dyson—have responded to rap's disturbing elements in a way that attempts to understand the logic and motivations behind these facets of its expressions.

The aesthetic complexity of some of the lyrics by prominent hardcore (some say gangsta) rappers such as Snoop Doggy Dog, Scarface from the Geto Boys, and Ice Cube and the genius of the best music that accompanies it almost always are overlooked completely in the attacks on rap, in part out of genuine ignorance (similar dismissals have clung to the reception of all black American music, jazz included), and in part because exploring these facets of rap's lure would damage the process of creating easily identifiable villains.

Basically, reality is more complicated than the current crime debate allows. Who would we blame, if not rappers and their fans? Rap music has become a lightning rod for those politicians and law and order officials who are hell-bent on scapegoating it as a major source of violence instead of attending to the much more difficult and complicated work of transforming the brutally unjust institutions that shape the lives of poor people. Attacking rap during this so-called crisis of crime and violence is a facile smokescreen that protects the real culprits and deludes the public into believing that public officials are taking a bite out of crime. In the face of daunting economic and social conditions that are felt most severely by the young people they represent, rappers are cast as the perpetrators.

Chronicling Blacks' Experience

Some hardcore rap no doubt is producing images and ideas that I, among many others, find troubling and saddening. This is not to be interpreted as a denial or defense of rap's problematic elements. At the same time and in equal amounts, many rappers are able to codify the everyday experiences of demonized young black men and bear witness to the experiences they face, never see explained from their perspective, but know are true. Many a gangsta rap tale chronicles the experience of wandering around all day, trying to make order out of a horizon of unemployment, gang cultural occupation, the threat of violence from police and rival teens, and fragile home relationships.

Given this complexity in rap's storytelling, how is it that most Americans only know about the most extremely violent passages? What does it mean to vilify rap in the face of the profound social and economic dispossession that consumes poor communities today? How can a black leader like Rev. Calvin Butts make his media name on attacking a cultural form he exhibits so little knowledge about? How can black representatives, such as Representative Cardiss Collins

> *"Rap music has become a lightning rod for those . . . who are hell-bent on scapegoating it as a major source of violence."*

(D.-Ill.) and Senator Carol Moseley-Braun (D.-Ill.), hold a series of Congressional and Senatorial hearings on gangsta rap under the Sub-committees on Commerce and Consumer Protection and Youth and Urban Crime, respectively, when life and death matters of social and political justice that face Chicago's black teens remain unscheduled for public scrutiny? These hearings are a form of empty moral grandstanding, a shameful attempt by politicians to earn political favors and ride the wave of public frenzy about crime while at the same time remaining unable and often unwilling to tackle the real problems that plague America's cities and their poorest black children.

Hip hop culture and rap music have become the cultural emblem for America's young black city kids, only a small percentage of which participate in street crimes. The more public opinion, political leaders, and policymakers criminalize hip hop as the cultural example of a criminal way of thinking, the more imaginary black monsters will surface. In this fearful fantasy, hip hop style (or whatever style young black men create and adopt) becomes a code for criminal behavior, and censuring the music begins to look more and more like fighting crime.

Rap Music Should Not Be Censored

by Barbara Ehrenreich

About the author: *Barbara Ehrenreich is the author of several books, includ-ing* Kipper's Game, Fear of Falling: The Inner Life of the Middle Class, *and* The Worst Years of Our Lives: Irreverent Notes from a Decade of Greed. *She is a frequent contributor to* Time *and other national magazines.*

Ice-T's song "Cop Killer" is as bad as they come. This is black anger—raw, rude and cruel—and one reason the song's so shocking is that in postliberal America, black anger is virtually taboo. You won't find it on TV, not on the *McLaughlin Group* or *Crossfire*, and certainly not in the placid features of Ar-senio Hall or Bernard Shaw. It's been beaten back into the outlaw subcultures of rap and rock, where, precisely because it is taboo, it sells. And the nastier it is, the faster it moves off the shelves. As Ice-T asks in another song on the same album, "Goddamn what a brotha gotta do/ To get a message through/ To the red, white and blue?"

A Gross Overreaction

But there's a gross overreaction going on, building to a veritable paroxysm of white denial. A national boycott has been called, not just of the song or Ice-T, but of all Time Warner products. The President himself has denounced Time Warner as "wrong" and Ice-T as "sick." Ollie North's Freedom Alliance has started a petition drive aimed at bringing Time Warner executives to trial for "sedition and anarchy."

Much of this is posturing and requires no more courage than it takes to stand up in a VFW hall and condemn communism or crack. Yes, "Cop Killer" is irre-sponsible and vile. But Ice-T is as right about some things as he is righteous about the rest. And ultimately, he's not even dangerous—least of all to the white power structure his songs condemn.

The "danger" implicit in all the uproar is of empty-headed, suggestible black kids, crouching by their boom boxes, waiting for the word. But what Ice-T's fans know and his detractors obviously don't is that "Cop Killer" is just one more entry in pop music's long history of macho hyperbole and violent boast. Flip to the classic-rock station, and you might catch the Rolling Stones announcing "the time is right for violent revo-loo-shun!" from their 1968 hit "Street Fighting Man." And where were the defenders of our law-enforcement officers when a white British group, the Clash, taunted its fans with the lyrics: "When they kick open your front door/ How you gonna come/ With your hands on your head/ Or on the trigger of your gun?"

"Die, Die, Die Pig" is strong speech, but the Constitution protects strong speech, and it's doing so this year more aggressively than ever. The Supreme Court has just downgraded cross burnings to the level of bonfires and ruled that it's no crime to throw around verbal grenades like "nigger" and "kike." Where are the defenders of decorum and social stability when prime-time demagogues like Howard Stern deride African Americans as "spear chuckers"?

African Americans Are Not Naïve

More to the point, young African Americans are not so naive and suggestible that they have to depend on a compact disc for their sociology lessons. To paraphrase another song from another era, you don't need a rap song to tell which way the wind is blowing. Black youths know that the police are likely to see them through a filter of stereotypes as miscreants and potential "cop killers." They are aware that a black youth is seven times as likely to be charged with a felony as a white youth who has committed the same offense, and is much more likely to be imprisoned.

> *"Yes, 'Cop-Killer' is irresponsible and vile. But Ice-T is as right about some things as he is righteous about the rest."*

They know, too, that in a shameful number of cases, it is the police themselves who indulge in "anarchy" and violence. The U.S. Justice Department has received 47,000 complaints of police brutality in the past six years, and Amnesty International has just issued a report on police brutality in Los Angeles, documenting 40 cases of "torture or cruel, inhuman or degrading treatment."

Menacing as it sounds, the fantasy in "Cop Killer" is the fantasy of the powerless and beaten down—the black man who's been hassled once too often ("A pig stopped me for nothin'!"), spread-eagled against a police car, pushed around. It's not a "responsible" fantasy (fantasies seldom are). It's not even a very creative one. In fact, the sad thing about "Cop Killer" is that it falls for the cheapest, most conventional image of rebellion that our culture offers: the lone gunman spraying fire from his AK-47. This is not "sedition"; it's the familiar, all-American, Hollywood-style pornography of violence.

Which is why Ice-T is right to say he's no more dangerous than George

Bush's pal Arnold Schwarzenegger, who wasted an army of cops in *Terminator 2*. Images of extraordinary cruelty and violence are marketed every day, many of far less artistic merit than "Cop Killer." This is our free market of ideas and images, and it shouldn't be any less free for a black man than for other purveyors of "irresponsible" sentiments, from David Duke to Andrew Dice Clay.

Just, please, don't dignify Ice-T's contribution with the word sedition. The past masters of sedition—men like George Washington, Toussaint-Louverture, Fidel Castro or Mao Zedong, all of whom led and won armed insurrections—would be unimpressed by "Cop Killer" and probably saddened. They would shake their heads and mutter words like "infantile" and "adventurism." They might point out that the cops are hardly a noble target, being, for the most part, honest working stiffs who've got stuck with the job of patrolling ghettos ravaged by economic decline and official neglect.

There is a difference, the true seditionist would argue, between a revolution and a gesture of macho defiance. Gestures are cheap. They feel good, they blow off some rage. But revolutions, violent or otherwise, are made by people who have learned how to count very slowly to 10.

Rap Musicians Contribute Positively to Society

by Maria Armoudian

About the author: *Maria Armoudian is a contributor to* Billboard *magazine.*

While so much emphasis is placed on the detrimental effects of some rap music, there's little acknowledgment of rap's positive cultural contribution and social activism.

Jive's KRS-One, known to his community as "The Teacher," is just one example of the good work being done. Once homeless, KRS-One now lectures at such universities as Harvard, Yale, Vassar and Stanford on his philosophies. "The deepest part of being black is being African. The deepest part of being African is being human," he has stated. "The deepest part of being human is being universal. And the deepest part of being universal is being balanced. It is all according to where you start or stop studying."

The rap artist has been actively involved with such organizations as Stop the Violence, HEAL and the National Urban League (for which he raised $600,000). One of KRS-One's newer projects, "Break the Chain," the debut of Marvel Music's new multimedia line, features an audiocassette soundtrack with three KRS-One songs as well as spoken-word. It's accompanied by a glossy 32-page color comic book that kids can use to follow along. The project promotes literacy and cultural awareness and teaches black history.

Public Enemy Is a Good Ally

In the forefront of rap activism is Public Enemy, particularly leader Chuck D. Though sometimes criticized for excessively violent lyrics, Public Enemy's intentions ostensibly have been to elevate the morale and circumstances of their community.

The group launched a Black Awareness Program to heighten media awareness of important black issues and to strengthen and uplift the black community through education and positive works. The members also have raised or con-

Maria Armoudian, "Rap: Beating the Bad Rap," *Billboard*, November 26, 1994.

tributed money for various causes, such as the Urban Development Program, a nationwide program by which youths build houses for homeless. And while on a fact-finding mission/concert tour of South Africa/Azania, Public Enemy donated a percentage of its profits to numerous South African liberation movements, such as the African National Congress and Azanian People's Organization.

> *"There's little acknowledgment of rap's positive cultural contribution and social activism."*

Back in the States, Public Enemy toured 20 cities in the Unity for Peace tour and raised money for such local charities as the Boys and Girls clubs. Chuck D frequently speaks about issues of empowerment in numerous forums, including universities, juvenile homes and correctional facilities, and supports many community organizations, such as Empowerment for Hartford's Youth.

Adamantly opposed to alcohol advertisement in the black communities, Chuck D has led the fight to end them. For his extensive work, he was named Black History Maker of the Year by *Urban Profile* magazine.

Eazy-E participates with charity groups Athletes & Entertainers for Children and the Make A Wish Foundation, but his favorite cause is his own hometown of Compton, California. Eazy-E has met with Mayor Tom Bradley, and the two have initiated a working relationship, concluding mutual goals for the city. The rapper filmed and narrated a public-service announcement on fire safety for the Compton Fire Department, for which he recruited rapper Brownside. He also made—and funded—a Spanish version of the PSA for the city's Latino community.

Working for Their Communities

There are many other rap artists working to better their communities, whether by getting involved with charitable organizations or by speaking out about political issues.

Rap group The Coup organized the Mau Mau Rhythm Collective, which includes artists, educators and activists, as a means to lobby for various local causes, organize protests and conduct readings and study groups that focus on African-American history and politics. The members of The Coup also speak in schools and local community centers, emphasizing topics related to exploitation and oppression, according to the group's MC Boots.

Rapper D.J. Woody Wood of Three Times Dope (3XD) is the project coordinator for Youth Outreach Adolescent Community AIDS Project (YO ACAP), an affiliate of the Greater Philadelphia Urban Affairs Coalition. Wood also founded the Celebrity AIDS Awareness Project (CAAP), a national AIDS education program that involves the participation of popular rap artists in an effort to teach adolescents about the disease.

Doug E Fresh is a spokesperson for Voter Jam 94, a campaign sponsored by the New York State Association of Black and Puerto Rican Legislators. The campaign is intended to increase voter registration among black and Latino youth in New York. He works with the New York Board of Education and frequently speaks at high schools and community colleges on issues of confidence and self-esteem.

Ahmad speaks at schools and centers such as Ofman Learning Center, where runaways and gang members try to make a fresh start. And the group Grave Diggaz also can be found talking to kids at schools and youth centers.

Hardcore rapper MC Eiht participates in various activities, performing and playing benefit basketball games with well-known athletes to benefit youth centers, recreation centers and gang-truce organizations, such as The Truce Foundation in Las Vegas.

Positive Labels

Rap record companies, too, are joining the positive efforts. Dangerous Records, for instance, uses the rap genre to promote peace. The recently released "Bangin' on Wax—The Saga Continues" is the second effort recorded by members of both the Bloods and Crips gangs. The record "demystified gang colors and gang slang—brought them into the light," says Dangerous president Ronnie Phillips.

> *"These street warriors are teaching gang members everywhere that they can deal with their violence without acting it out."*

"These street warriors are teaching gang members everywhere that they can deal with their violence without acting it out." Phillips' efforts have led to recording careers for a few of the gang member rappers on the album. He has also donated $5,000 to the Stamps Youth Foundation, a Los Angeles–based organization that works with gang members trying to change their lives.

Another label, Priority Records, has joined with Los Angeles radio station Power 106 to compile an album that will help fund the building of a performing-arts center. Participating artists include Sir Mix-A-Lot, Tag Team, Rodney O & Joe Cooley, House Of Pain, Black Sheep, Paperboy, Digable Planets, Ice Cube, N2Deep, Dr. Dre, Doz Effects, Public Enemy and George Clinton—all of whom are donating their performances and royalties.

Bibliography

Books

Ken Auletta
Three Blind Mice: How the TV Networks Lost Their Way. New York: Random House, 1991.

Robert K. Avery and David Eason, eds.
Critical Perspectives on Media and Society. New York: Guilford Press, 1991.

Steven J. Bennett
Kick the TV Habit: A Simple Program for Changing Your Family's Television Viewing and Video Game Habits. New York: Penguin, 1994.

David Bianculli
Teleliteracy: Taking Television Seriously. New York: Continuum, 1994.

George Comstock
Television and the American Child. San Diego, CA: Academic Press, 1991.

Douglas Davis
The Five Myths of Television Power, or Why the Medium Is Not the Message. New York: Simon & Schuster, 1993.

Jib Fowles
Why Viewers Watch: A Reappraisal of Television's Effects. Newbury Park, CA: Sage, 1992.

Barbara Hattemer and Robert Showers
Don't Touch That Dial: The Impact of the Media on Children and the Family. Lafayette, LA: Huntington House, 1993.

Aletha Huston et al.
Big World, Small Screen: The Role of Television in American Society. Lincoln: University of Nebraska Press, 1992.

S. Robert Lichter, Linda S. Lichter, and Stanley Rothman
Watching America: What Television Tells Us About Our Lives. New York: Prentice Hall, 1991.

Michael Medved
Hollywood vs. America: Popular Culture and the War on Traditional Values. New York: HarperCollins, 1992.

Andrea L. Press
Women Watching Television: Gender, Class, and Generation in the American Television Experience. Philadelphia: University of Pennsylvania Press, 1991.

Joan Anderson Wilkins
Breaking the TV Habit. New York: Scribner, 1992.

J. Mallory Wober
Television and Social Control. New York: St. Martin's Press, 1988.

Bibliography

Periodicals

Advertising Age   "Say No to Censors," July 12, 1993. Available from 965 E. Jefferson Ave., Detroit, MI 48207-3185.

Martin Amis   "Blown Away," *The New Yorker*, May 30, 1994.

Ken Auletta   "The Electronic Parent," *The New Yorker*, November 8, 1993.

Ken Auletta   "What Won't They Do? Annals of Communications," *The New Yorker*, May 17, 1993.

Philip J. Auter   "The Relationship Between Watching Violent Programming and Acting in a Socially Destructive Manner Is Dubious at Best," *Broadcasting & Cable*, August 16, 1993. Available from Box 6399, Torrance, CA 90504.

Russell Baker   "Busby Goes Berserk," *The New York Times*, July 3, 1993.

David Durenberger   "I See No Reason We Should Not Warn Parents About the Harmful Effects That TV Violence May Have on Their Children," *Broadcasting & Cable*, May 31, 1993.

The Economist   "Child-Minders: Film Censors," August 13, 1994.

The Economist   "Videodrome," August 13, 1994.

Kay Gardella   "Violence on the Home Screen," *America*, September 1, 1993.

Walter Goodman   "Qualifying the Quantity of On-Screen Violence," *The New York Times*, August 30, 1994.

Meg Greenfield   "TV's True Violence," *Newsweek*, June 21, 1993.

Owen Husney   "Hardcore Rappers Are Voice of the Underclass," *Billboard*, June 27, 1992. Available from 1515 Broadway, New York, NY 10036.

Laurence Jarvik   "Violence in Pursuit of Justice Is No Vice," *Insight on the News*, December 19, 1994. Available from 3600 New York Ave. NE, Washington, DC 20002.

Dean Koontz   "Why We Love Horror," *TV Guide*, October 23, 1993.

Steve Kurtz   "Deja Viewing," *Reason*, February 1994.

Steve Kurtz   "Sensitive Censors: The Ubiquity of Uniquity," *Reason*, July 1994.

Lewis Lapham   "Burnt Offerings," *Harper's Magazine*, April 1994.

John Leo   "One Poke over the Line," *U.S. News & World Report*, October 26, 1992.

S. Robert Lichter   "Bam! Whoosh! Crack! TV Worth Squelching," *Insight on the News*, December 19, 1994.

Michael Medved   "Hollywood's Fascination with Filth," *Reader's Digest*, October 1992.

Tom Morganthau   "Can TV Violence Be Curbed?" *Newsweek*, November 1, 1993.

Havelock Nelson   "Music and Violence: Does Crime Pay? 'Gangsta' Gunplay Sparks Industry Debate," *Billboard*, November 13, 1993.

Jon Pareles   "Can Good Guys Challenge Gangster Rap?" *The New York Times*, June 12, 1994.

Peter Plagens   "Violence in Our Culture," *Newsweek*, April 1, 1991.

Virginia I. Postrel   "TV or Not TV?" *Reason*, August/September 1993.

Ron Rosenbaum   "The Evil Movies Do: Violent Flicks May Hurt Women Both on and off the Screen," *Mademoiselle*, February 1991.

Roger Rosenblatt   "Shadow on the Wall," *Family Circle*, January 12, 1993.

Steve S. Salem   "Rap Music Mirrors Its Environment," *Billboard*, November 27, 1993.

David Samuels   "The Rap on Rap: The 'Black Music' That Isn't Either," *The New Republic*, November 11, 1991.

Gene Siskel   "Tuning Out the Violence," *Parenting*, December 1992/January 1993.

Michael Small   "Rap's Bad Rap," *Vogue*, March 1993.

Danyel Smith   "House of Pain: The Fight Against Gangsta Rap Hits Capitol Hill," *Rolling Stone*, April 7, 1994.

David S. Toolan   "Voyeurs of Savage Fury," *America*, April 27, 1991.

Tevi Troy   "Faster, Hollywood! Kill! Kill!" *Reason*, July 1992.

Francis Wilkinson   "More Washington Show Talk: In Today's Episode, TV Ruins Everything," *Rolling Stone*, December 9, 1993.

Organizations to Contact

The editors have compiled the following list of organizations concerned with the issues debated in this book. The descriptions are derived from materials provided by the organizations. All have publications or information available for interested readers. The list was compiled on the date of publication of the present volume; names, addresses, and phone numbers may change. Be aware that many organizations take several weeks or longer to respond to inquiries, so allow as much time as possible.

American Family Association
PO Drawer 2440
Tupelo, MS 38803
(601) 844-5036

The association opposes the portrayal of anything violent, immoral, profane, or vulgar on television or in the movies. It sponsors letter-writing campaigns and compiles statistics on how media violence affects society. The association's publications include reports and the monthly newsletter *AFA Journal*.

Center for Media and Public Affairs
2101 L St. NW, Suite 405
Washington, DC 20037
(202) 223-2942
fax: (202) 872-4014

The center studies the way the media addresses social and political issues. As part of this task, the center uses surveys to discover how the media affect public opinion. The organization publishes the monthly *Media Monitor*, the monograph *A Day of Television Violence*, and other monographs, books, and articles.

Fairness and Accuracy in Reporting (FAIR)
130 W. 25th St.
New York, NY 10001
(212) 633-6700
fax: (212) 727-7668

FAIR is a media watchdog organization. It believes that the media are controlled by and support government and corporate interests while ignoring issues that affect women, minorities, labor, and other special-interest groups. FAIR publishes the periodical *EXTRA!* and the books *Unreliable Sources* and *Adventures in Medialand*. It also produces the nationally syndicated radio show *Counterspin*.

Freedom Forum Media Studies Center
2950 Broadway
New York, NY 10027-7004
(212) 280-8392

The center is a research organization dedicated to studying the media and educating the public about its influence on society. It publishes numerous conference reports and papers, including *The Media and Women*.

Free Press Association
PO Box 15548
Columbus, OH 43215
(614) 291-1441

The association is an international network of journalists, editors, publishers, writers, and artists committed to combating all censorship of the media. It works to educate the public concerning the importance of a free media. The association monitors and reports on issues and judicial cases affecting First Amendment rights. Its publications include the quarterly *Free Press Network*.

Media Action Research Center
475 Riverside Dr., Suite 1901
New York, NY 10115
(212) 865-6690
fax: (212) 663-2746

The center provides resources and information to educate the public concerning the affect of television on viewers. It seeks to reduce violence and sex on television. The center holds workshops and offers the course "Growing with Television: A Study of Biblical Values and the Television Experience." Its publications include the quarterly *Media and Values* and leaflets, packets, and program guidebooks.

Media Research Center
113 S. West St.
Alexandria, VA 22314
(703) 683-9733
fax: (703) 683-9736

The center is a conservative media watchdog organization that documents what it perceives as liberal bias in the news and entertainment media. It publishes the monthly newsletters *Media Watch*, which focuses on the news media, and *TV, Etc.*, which examines the entertainment media.

Morality in Media
475 Riverside Dr.
New York, NY 10115
(212) 870-3222

Morality in Media opposes what it considers to be indecent in broadcasting—especially pornography. It works to educate and organize the public in support of strict decency laws and has launched an annual "turn off the TV" day to protest offensive television programming. It publishes the *Morality in Media Newsletter* and the handbook *TV: The World's Greatest Mind-Bender*.

National Coalition Against Censorship
275 Seventh Ave., 20th Fl.
New York, NY 10001
(212) 807-6222
fax: (212) 807-6245

The coalition opposes censorship in any form, believing it to be against the First Amendment right to freedom of speech. It works to educate the public about the dangers of censorship, including censorship of violence on television and in movies and music. The coalition publishes *Censorship News* five times a year and reports such as *The Sex Panic: Women, Censorship, and "Pornography."*

National Coalition on Television Violence
33290 W. 14 Mile Rd., Suite 498
West Bloomfield, MI 48322
(810) 489-3177

The coalition is an educational and research organization committed to decreasing the amount of violence on television and in films. It sponsors speakers and seminars and publishes ratings and reviews of films and television programs. The coalition produces reports, educational materials, and the *NCTV Journal.*

National Council for Families and Television
3801 Barham Blvd., Suite 300
Los Angeles, CA 90068
(213) 876-5959

The council includes television producers, writers, and executives as well as advertisers, educators, child development and family life specialists, pediatricians, psychologists, and anthropologists. These professionals work together to change television programming to be more beneficial for families and children. The council conducts seminars and publishes the monthly *NCFT Information Service Bulletin* and the quarterly *Television and Families.*

Society for the Eradication of Television (SET)
Box 10491
Oakland, CA 94610-0491
(510) 763-8712

SET members oppose television and encourage others to stop all television viewing. The society believes television "retards the inner life of human beings, destroys human interaction, and squanders time." SET maintains a speakers bureau and reference library and publishes manuals and pamphlets, the periodic *Propaganda War Comix,* and the quarterly *SET Free: The Newsletter Against Television.*

Strategies for Media Literacy
1095 Market St., Suite 617
San Francisco, CA 94103
(415) 621-2911
fax: (415) 255-2298

Strategies for Media Literacy works to educate the public about the effects of television, movies, and other media on society. It promotes the concept of media literacy, whereby viewers gain an awareness and understanding of how advertisers and others in the media are trying to influence them. The organization publishes the video *The Critical Eye: Inside TV Advertising,* the book *Media and You: An Elementary Media Literacy Curriculum,* and the quarterly *Strategies.*

Index

Index

Index

Metzenbaum, Howard, 120, 132
Miami Vice (TV series), 108
Midnight Express (film), 103
Mighty Mouse (TV series), 48
Miller, Henry, 134
Mississippi Burning (film), 122
Mister Rogers' Neighborhood (TV series), 91
Moseley-Braun, Carol, 164, 173
Mother Jones (magazine), 40, 41, 46
Motion Picture Association of America, 99
Motion Picture Code, 86, 150
Motley Crüe, 153, 157
movies
    rating system is ineffective, 98-100
    on television, 77, 106-108, 112
    violence in, 17-18
        causes violent crime, 20-21
        desensitizes males, 20, 63
        has been reduced, 81, 82, 84
            con, 101-104
MTV (Music Television)
    and *Beavis and Butt-Head*, 66
    influence of, 150-51, 157
    rap music on, 156
    regulation of, 158
    rejection of videos by, 80
    violence on, 131
murder
    television contributes to, 19-20, 25-26, 54, 115
        con, 46, 67
Murder in the Heartland (TV film), 77
Murphy, Thomas S., 27
Murphy Brown (TV series), 133
My Lai massacre, 103
Mystery Science Theater 3000 (TV series), 48

Nasty Savage, 155
National Center for Juvenile Justice, 143
National Center for Missing and Exploited
    Children (NCMEC), 87
National Coalition on Television Violence, 71
    on rock videos, 154
    on violence in television, 49, 111-12, 117
National Commission on Violence, 118
National Endowment for the Arts (NEA), 136
National Foundation to Improve Television, 113,
    114, 116
National Institute of Mental Health, 26
National Rifle Association (NRA), 18, 30
    and television violence, 25, 27, 76
National Task Force on TV Violence, 58
Natural Born Killers (film), 81
NBC-TV
    news programs, 107, 118
    rejection of violent shows, 77, 81
    study of violence, 19
New Jersey, assault weapons ban in, 30
Newsweek, 156
New York Times, 96
New Zealand, television regulations in, 113
Nightmare on Elm Street (film), 21
North, Oliver, 175
Northern Exposure (TV series), 35

NYPD Blue (TV series), 63, 74, 81, 107

Olmos, Edward James, 80
One False Move (film), 101, 102, 103, 104
Operation PUSH, 164
Osbourne, Ozzy, 153, 154, 155
Over Easy (TV series), 91

Paglia, Camille, 137
Paramount Television, 80
parental advisories, 70
    establishment of, 68, 99, 140
    help protect children, 140
        con, 71, 74-75, 115-16, 132-133, 135, 138
    on video games, 124
Parents' Music Resource Center (PMRC), 135
Phillips, Kevin, 134, 141
Picket Fences (TV series), 35
Pilger, John, 101
Pink Floyd, 154
Plato, 50
police brutality, 176
pornography, 134, 155-56
Postrel, Virginia I., 70
poverty, 103
    relation to television watching, 63
    relation to violent crime, 145, 170
Prince, 155
Program, The (film), 46
Project Censored, 167
Prothrow-Stith, Deborah, 131, 147
Psychological Bulletin, 40
Public Broadcasting Service (PBS), 49, 68, 89
Public Enemy, 178-179
Public Interest, 54

Quayle, Dan, 65, 75, 133, 141
Queen Latifah, 164

racism, 166
radio
    influence on children, 50, 150-51
    and rap music, 162, 163-64, 167-168
Rainie, Harrison, 74
Raising PG Kids in an X-Rated Society (Gore),
    135
Rakolta, Terry, 70-71, 124, 135, 138
Rambo (film), 21
rap music
    positive contributions of, 178-80
    promotes violence, 156-57
        against blacks, 159-62
            con, 169-74
        against women, 163-65
    should be censored, 166-68
        con, 175-77
Reagan, Ronald, 46, 118, 125
Redford, Robert, 17
Reno, Janet, 44
    boycott recommendation, 120
    congressional testimony on, 39, 62, 83
    constitutionality of regulation, 39, 109
    and television violence

190